# Advance Praise for *How to Get the Death You Want*

"John Abraham's huge experience with end-of-life issues makes this book a veritable encyclopedia of the subject. There isn't any aspect which he had not come across, thus addressed here are all the quirky and remote matters that tend to crop up at the close of life's journey. The book is a clear and fast read, provocative and informative."

— Derek Humphry, founder of the Hemlock Society, author of *Final Exit*

"Whatever your opinions on the right-to-die movement, this is a book you must have in your library. It will help you unlock the complexities of this controversial subject with a treasure trove of creative insights and practical understanding. Provocative, evocative, and fearless, yet it is very readable with John Abraham's warmth and humor. Highly recommended!"

— Rabbi Earl A. Grollman, DHL, DD, Author of *Living When a Loved One has Died* and numerous other best-selling books on death, grieving, and related topics

"Many people do not want to talk about death for a single minute. John has been talking about it, studying it, and writing about it for forty-five years. He knows the subject. In those forty-five years (and I have known John for all forty-five of them) his knowledge has evolved and his passion has grown in a particular direction: wanting all of us to have just as much freedom in dying as we have in living. This, his latest publication, shows us, with all of John's knowledge and all of his passion, how we can have that freedom. If you want such freedom, you need to read this book and study it."

— Douglas Smith, M.Div., M.A., M.S., author of *The Tao of Dying* and *The Complete Book of Counseling the Dying and the Grieving*

"Any who are nearing the end of life, or who have loved ones with illnesses that may soon end their life, will find a wealth of information in this book. John Abraham brings such practical advice, written in accessible language, to the subject of preparing for dying. His decades of experience as a counselor to those near the end of life, supported by his actually having been with some who chose their own time of dying, makes the information he provides credible and valuable."

— Richard MacDonald, M.D., Medical Director, Hemlock Society, 1993–2004; Senior Medical Adviser, Final Exit Network, 2005–2015; President, World Federation of Right To Die Societies, 2000–2002

"Episcopal Priest John L. Abraham has never shied away from controversy. During his years of innovative hospice practices and caring for the dying, he has too often witnessed unwilling patients being forced to go along with doctors who only prolonged their patients' suffering. This inspired him to speak up for a death with dignity for those who chose not to artificially prolong their painful and hopeless situation.

"Abraham has written this book about his experiences and it includes horror stories of those who did not get the death they wanted, and describes his efforts — both inside and outside the clergy — to ensure that government and health professionals listen to the wishes of those who choose a hastened death.

"This book is not for the faint of heart. Abraham does not mince words when describing what he has witnessed.

"And he gives detailed lists on what to do when dealing with family members, friends, clergy and medical professionals who may not share the reader's personal choices in their manner of dying. The book also has very helpful lists that will prove useful to anyone who ever has to plan a funeral or settle an estate.

"*How to Get the Death You Want* also explores physician aid in dying in the American states that now allow this, along with the more enlightened European countries who have less stringent requirements than the U.S. It truly is the ultimate "how to" book for the one process that all of us will one day go through. And it explains in a factual, logical and very clear and direct way the reasons why some of us join right-to-die organizations such as Hemlock, Compassion & Choices and Final Exit Network.

"Regardless of the reader's position on physician aid in dying, the various lists it contains by themselves make this a worthwhile book to own and read, even if only used to ensure that you are treated the way you want during a hospital or nursing home stay."

— Renée Neumann, Final Exit Network member, Tucson, Arizona

"Freedom of choice, and the right to control one's own body, continue to be among the greatest struggles of our time. In this book, John Abraham strongly advocates for the right of people to choose a dignified and pain-free ending to the relentless suffering that so often turns the end of life into a prolonged nightmare. Importantly, he gives individuals, and their advocates, the information and tools they will need to navigate the legal and medical systems, and achieve that goal."

— Lisa Carlson, executive director, Funeral Ethics Organization,
co-author of *Final Rights: Reclaiming the American Way of Death*

# HOW TO GET THE DEATH YOU WANT

## Disclaimers

Opinions expressed in this book are those of the author, not reviewed for endorsement by any of the organizations referred to in the book or by the publisher, Upper Access Books. Legal and factual information has been carefully researched but cannot be guaranteed and cannot substitute for consultation with a lawyer, physician, or other expert who is knowledgeable about your specific circumstances.

Upper Access titles are available at special discounts for bulk purchases. Please contact the publisher to inquire. For such inquiries, contact Steve Carlson, *steve@upperaccess.com*, or 802-482-2988

# HOW TO GET THE DEATH YOU WANT

## A Practical and Moral Guide

John Abraham

Upper Access Books
Hinesburg, Vermont
*www.upperaccess.com*

Published by Upper Access Books
87 Upper Access Road, Hinesburg, Vermont 05461
(802) 482-2988 • *http://www.upperaccess.com*



Design of cover and interior layout by Kitty Werner.

ISBN: 978-0-942679-40-3

---

Library of Congress Cataloging-in-Publication Data

Names: Abraham, John (Episcopal priest), author.
Title: How to get the death you want : a practical and moral guide / John Abraham.
Description: Hinesburg, Vermont : Upper Access Books, [2017] | Includes bibliographical references.
Identifiers: LCCN 2016046550 | ISBN 9780942679403 (alk. paper)
Subjects: LCSH: Terminally ill. | Terminal care. | Thanatology.
Classification: LCC R726.8 .A27 2017 | DDC 616.02/9--dc23
LC record available at https://lccn.loc.gov/2016046550

Printed on acid-free paper in the United States of America

17 / 10 9 8 7 6 5 4 3 2 1

# Acknowledgments

Throughout my four decades of teaching death education, one salient factor stands out: I have learned far more than I ever taught. To my students, fellow supporters in the right-to-die movement (especially members of Final Exit Network), participants in my various workshops and classes, I am most grateful.

> The dead teach this great lesson, which we are loathe to learn: we too will die.
>
> — John Updike

And I am grateful to others who have supported me, inspired me, encouraged me to take risks, and helped me to think "outside the box." (Yes, I am a card-carrying member of "The Giraffe Society" for those who stick their necks out.) A few who come to mind over the years are my parents, Maurice and Joan Abraham; The Reverend Doug Smith; The Right Reverend John Walker, Bishop of Washington, D.C.; The Reverend Jo Tartt, Jr.; Rabbi Earl Grollman; The Reverend John Fletcher; The Reverend Bill Wendt; and Derek Humphry. And it was the Bishop of Atlanta, The Right Reverend Bennett Sims, who when I consulted him about my having some conflict difficulties with a congregation assured me: "There is always hope. People die."

And I give thanks for J'Fleur and Tim Lohman, Steve Carlson, and Jeri Helen Belisle, who have been most supportive, been ever so patient, and greatly helped me to organize this effort.

# Dedication

I dedicate this book to my beloved children, Katharine (Katie) and Paul. Both have endured life's struggles and are now doing well. May they have life in all its fullness and prosper.

And I am grateful to all with whom I have worked in exploring death and dying, especially many who were near life's end and taught me so much.

# Contents

Douglas C. Smith

# Foreword

Many people do not want to talk about death for a single minute. John Abraham has been talking about it, studying it, and writing about it for forty-five years. He knows about the subject from multiple directions and points of view, directions and points of view typically not explored by other authors. In those forty-five years of exploration (and I have known John for all forty-five of them) his knowledge has evolved and his passion around the topic of dying and death has grown in a particular direction: wanting everyone to be able to exercise just as much freedom in dying as they have in living. In *How to Get the Death You Want*, John, with all of his knowledge and his passion, shows all of us how we can have that freedom.

In this book, John not only shares his own wisdom, but also summarizes the wisdom of numerous physicians, psychotherapists, and other healthcare providers who are also experts in the field of caring for the terminally ill. In addition, his text is overflowing with poignant and relevant quotations from many other sources: from Walt Whitman to Kurt Vonnegut, from Sarah Bernhardt to Morgan Freeman, from Swami Satchidananda to the Dalai Lama to Episcopal Bishop John Spong.

Without sugarcoating anything, John "tells it like it is," not skirting around any issues or avoiding any questions. In doing such, he makes *How To Get The Death You Want* not only an informative book but also a very practical one as well, giving practical advice for the dying, their families, their friends and their caregivers — from the moment of learning of the terminal diagnosis to the very moment of death.

John's a very down-to-earth kind of guy. He doesn't mess around with the trivial. He centers in on what's really important, the meaty stuff, but he can do it with a sense of humor, not taking himself or the world too seriously. John has had to face life's ups and downs, and he has done it as a survivor; and he has learned some things he can give to others to help them be survivors also.

For any of you who are willing to admit that you will die and/or willing to admit that someone you know will die, I recommend this book. There is information here that, when the time comes, you will want to know.

— Douglas C. Smith, M.Div., MA, MS, author of *The Tao of Dying; Caregiving: Hospice Proven Techniques for Healing Body and Soul; The Complete Book of Counseling the Dying and the Grieving.*

# Introduction

*Whoever teaches people how to die, teaches them how to live!*
— Michel de Montaigne

At the outset, please know that this is not a religious book. It is for people of all faiths or no faith. Despite my identification as an Episcopal Priest, I am no longer active in that capacity, and in my work with the dying, their beliefs are important, not mine.

Might you suffer from Thanatophobia? Benjamin Franklin wrote in a 1789 letter that "our new Constitution is now established, and has an appearance that promises permanency; but in this world nothing can be said to be certain, except death and taxes." Nearly three million Americans will die this year.

As a thanatologist, I have been working with issues of death and dying for over forty years. Thanatology is the study of death-related issues. The term comes from Greek mythology, wherein we find twin brothers Hypnos and Thanatos, respectively the gods of sleep and of death. As John Steinbeck noted in *The Grapes of Wrath*, "Death was a friend, and sleep was Death's brother."

I regard death as a natural, rational, normal and inextricable part of life. We can't have one without the other. This ambigram is my logo:

For over a decade I have been teaching people how to get the death they want: explaining the difficulties of using advance directives and how to make sure their wishes are honored — not just for end of life care, but at any time they are in a medical institution. This book is meant to convey, and for you to gain, the desideratum that I offer. I hope my learnings are conveyed in a sufficiently pellucid way.

I have been propounding comprehensive training to be an Advocate/Surrogate/Proxy/Agent/ Health Care Representative (different terms in different U.S. states), discussing one's rights and options, and providing resources to help the ill and those they love to be prepared for the inevitable: death. Many have learned how to protect themselves, their loved ones, and others at a critical time of life. Now you can learn this too. I believe that being equipped with and acting on this knowledge is one of the best gifts you can give yourself, your loved ones, and your survivors.

In this book I argue for the right to die: for us to be free to determine how our lives will be completed when an individual is faced with a future that holds no promise. And I argue that the way most of us die these days is far from good. The tales of loved ones' deaths that I hear are nothing short of heartbreaking.

This issue could not be more timely, as various media pay more and more attention to such consideration, and more states enact right-to-die legislation. (Such legislation does not go far enough, though, as you will learn as your read on.)

> A small body of determined spirits fired by an unquenchable faith in their mission can alter the course of history.
>
> — Mahatma Gandhi

We have tried to introduce such legislation in Arizona for the past twenty years. I have joined other advocates in pleading for the right to die before the Arizona Legislature on several occasions. Twice we even took busloads of our supporters to champion our cause, parading with signs and speaking with legislators. On one of our sojourns to the Arizona Capital Dr. Merlin "Monte" DuVal, the founder of the University of Arizona's College of Medicine, accompanied me and put forth his argument that, since the state provides humane ways to execute criminals, it should also be able to open a "Death With Dignity Center" for those who desire a peaceful death. That was pretty bold.

> If life is pain, one could say that killing is an act of compassion. I look forward to my own death, you know. But dying is like losing your virginity. You can only do it once. I'm saving it for the right moment.
>
> — Amanda Steiger, *Dark Geist*

Now is the time for us to raise awareness of the right to die, especially as baby-boomers are becoming the aged. By 2030, an estimated 72 million Americans will be 65 or over, nearly one-fifth of the U.S. population. (*Newsweek* magazine actually reported on April 4, 2016 that adult diaper sales are forecast to rise by 48% by 2020.). Our nation's most populous state, California, granted the right to die to the terminally ill on June 9, 2016, becoming the fifth state to do so, and the media continue to raise the issue with ever greater frequency.

Some California hospitals have opted out of participating, claiming they cannot tell when someone will die. This is a specious argument if I ever heard one, since physicians have been pronouncing people "terminally ill" for decades as criteria for hospice admission. And there is a new front in the battle against death with dignity. Opponents are seeking to stop the laws in state courts after losing federal court cases filed in Oregon and Washington years ago. Now they are moving into state courts in California and Vermont, hoping they will get a different result. Make no mistake: the doctors and the anti-choice groups funding these lawsuits are political operatives attempting to derail the laws any way they can.

In spite of the grandeur of Washington D.C.'s Episcopal National Cathedral, or the majesty of many European cathedrals I have visited, I may echo the words of Jerome Lawrence who, in his play *Inherit the Wind* proclaimed that an idea is a greater monument than a cathedral. My idea is that the right to hasten one's death is the next great civil right.

Seeking some corroboration, in July of 2016 I emailed my friend, Morris Dees, the co-founder and chief trial counsel for the Southern Poverty Law Center, asking him whether he would endorse a statement that in the 21st century, we might add the "Right to a Death with Dignity" to the other ongoing struggles of recent decades—women's rights, racial rights, disability rights, and LGBT rights. He responded that he is "happy to endorse the statement of the Right to Death with Dignity."

Retired University of Arizona professor and fellow Final Exit Network member Timothy Lohman, who reviewed my early manuscript, commented that this book is unique in five ways.

1. Details on the steps after death of loved one from day one to one year: a great resource.
2. Why death is needed and the benefits: this aspect is rarely addressed.
3. How best to die: deliberate life completion. We rarely get good advice in this area.
4. Having an advocate: it is one thing to have all your wishes stated and filled out and on file…quite another to get them acted on. We all need an advocate at critical times in our dying process and John spells out all the details of what this entails.
5. Comprehensive perspective on the preparation for end of life from an experienced Thanatologist with so many examples of what is in store for each of us!

## My Background

My father was from England, and our family would visit his family members there regularly as well as tour throughout Europe. In England and elsewhere in Europe there were hospices long before any existed in the United States. Their idea of palliative care and easing the dying process made so much sense to me even as a youngster, I wondered why we didn't have it in this country.

So, in my early twenties, I helped start the third hospice in the U.S. in the mid 1970s in the Washington, D.C. area. Shortly thereafter, when I became pastor of a church near Montgomery, Alabama, I joined with Wanda Ruffin, a compassionate registered nurse, to found Hospice of Montgomery. The community was quite receptive to the concept and subsequently I did quite a bit of hospice training and consulting with fledgling hospices in several states. I have served hospices as president and in many other roles.

Hospice practices have changed significantly since we got started in Alabama. For example, Medicare did not pay for it then, and now one can get coverage for some medical interventions that were not permitted before.

I have seen virtually all manner of death and have simply seen too many people die badly. One of my first experiences with watching a person die was when I was twenty-seven. A young parishioner, Robert, was in intensive care after a horrific motorcycle accident. He was in his late twenties and barely clinging to life; severely battered and bandaged, with what seemed like endless tubes out of every orifice and several veins. He was drugged and plugged to the hilt, and his countenance was most disturbing. I remember well that when I saw him for the first time, upon leaving the hospital I did not get twenty feet beyond the exit before shaking and crying. His predicament was just too close to home; he was about my age, and I rode motorcycles in those days. I did not have the privilege of being with Robert when he died, but it was within a week of hospitalization. About twenty percent of us will end up in an intensive care unit at the end of life, and of those, about one-fourth will die there.

About a year after my experience with Robert's death I saw an elderly woman in the hospital who pleaded with me to help her die. She was suffering greatly, had led a good life, and just wanted out. At the time, there was nothing I could do to honor her wish. It turns out that these days if someone in a hospital tells a staff person that they want to die, they are largely ignored. It is anathema to most hospital personnel to let or to help someone die. Some think the person does not really mean what they're saying, or they just do not know how to reply.

Stephen P. Kiernan, the author of *Last Rights: Rescuing the End of Life From the Medical System*, says: "We found that health care professionals commonly did not respond to statements about wanting to die because they were worried they would say the wrong thing and further upset the patient, or because they were worried about professional or legal sanctions."

My experience as an Episcopal priest led me to believe that I would never want to suffer the way I saw so many people die: in isolation, abandoned and with great existential suffering. I would never want to be in an intensive care unit, hooked up to all kinds of machines. As a result, I began to look for a good way to die, knowing full well that dying is inevitable. Fortunately I met Derek Humphry in the late 1970s, joined the Hemlock Society in its first year of existence, and have been committed to helping others obtain a death with dignity ever since.

Although I am not an Exit Guide with Final Exit Network, I have been present for half a dozen exits by people using the helium method. They obtained the kind of death they wanted. And I have a friend who has been present with over two hundred such deaths. Both he and I would have to describe these experiences as both a privilege and a gift, because we are privileged that these people trust us, and we can be there with them and their family to witness such a significant event in their lives. It has meant that they should not have to die alone or miserable!

Having been raised in the Episcopal Church and having found it to be a good experience, I enrolled at Virginia Theological Seminary (VTS) in 1969. I was not enamored with it, but I stuck it out at VTS as a means to an end, and during the summer after my first year there I did six weeks of study at the Mid-Atlantic Career Center. This institution was not the kind of career center where at the end they pronounce "you should be hairdresser." It entailed a thorough inventory of my life's experiences with great emphasis on both enjoyments and accomplishments. My conclusion was that I would enjoy and be good at being an Episcopal priest. I enjoyed my chosen occupation. As for being good at it, you would have to ask others.

During seminary I had the good fortune of doing my field work with St. Stephen and the Incarnation Episcopal Church in Washington, D.C. under the direction and tutelage of The Reverend William (Bill) Wendt. The parish theme was "Celebrate Life," which is how I regard my involvement with death. To study death and dying may sound morbid. But truly my interest in this unusual topic is about making the most of the life we have and, in this case, the last part of that life. Bill Wendt was a rather radical priest, doing such things as using sacramental champagne and cookies instead of the customary red wine and unleavened bread wafer for Holy Communion at Easter.

Father Wendt was a somewhat unusual priest, and always an ardent advocate for the poor and dispossessed. He had begun a Memorial Society at St. Stephen's, and I joined this organization which sought to help people obtain affordable, ethical funerals. Today such groups are part of the Funeral Consumers Alliance (FCA), a nonprofit organization also dedicated to protecting a consumer's right to choose a meaningful, dignified, and affordable funeral. I have served on FCA's national board and currently serve on the Board of Directors of the Arizona chapter of the FCA. To accomplish its goals, FCA's services include:

- Offering pamphlets and newsletters on funeral choices to increase public awareness of funeral options, including how to care for your own dead without using a funeral home;
- Monitoring funeral industry trends and practices nationally and exposing abuses;
- Serving as a consumer advocate for legal and regulatory reform, giving advice on or lobbying for necessary changes locally, statewide, or nationally;
- Serving as a credible source of information for media covering death and dying;
- Working with national organizations sharing similar concerns to expand families' choices and control over funeral options;
- Giving advice and guidance to local memorial and funeral planning societies;
- Referring people to local funeral planning societies and regulatory agencies;
- Helping 100 funeral planning societies stay in touch with each other and exchange ideas.

Thanks to the FCA, it is now more difficult for funeral homes to engage in blatantly unethical or illegal practices, although there are still subtle forms of exploitation. For example, in display rooms the most expensive coffins are up front and well lit. And if one wants merely a cardboard container, one must ask for it. While I did not always accompany the grieving family to the funeral home, on one occasion in 1976 as the family selected an inexpensive coffin the funeral director told the family: "Well, we could fit him in this one, but we would have to break his legs to do it."

From St. Stephen's Memorial Society I bought my coffin in 1970. I use the word "coffin" deliberately. To me, a "casket" means a chest full of gold doubloons found with a shipwreck at the bottom of the ocean. I thought I would use it eventually, but since I plan to be cremated it will survive me. It is a simple pine box with rope handles, tapered around the shoulders in the wedge form or the traditional six-sided hexagonal kind of coffin. To this day it stands in my living room with the lower five shelves housing books about death and dying and the top shelf serving as a wine rack holding several bottles, and Earl the Dead Cat perched on top of the bottles. I use Earl in my classes about death-related humor. The lid, with six poly (vinyl chloride) legs attached, serves as my attention-getting coffee table.

## EARL THE DEAD CAT

In 1985 my wife and I celebrated our first Christmas as a married couple in our rented home in Tucson, Arizona without family and long-time friends. We were extra generous to each other and built upon each other's interests. I gave her a nicely framed quilt print, and she got me, much to my surprise and delight, Earl The Dead Cat. Waiting ever so patiently for me under the Christmas tree, there he was in sublime repose. Earl is a stuffed-toy dead cat, with flattened torso and sprawling limbs, about life-sized (or it is dead-sized?), with stitched crosses serving as lifeless eyes, his tongue hanging out of his mouth. He is billed as "the last cat you'll ever need."

Shortly after Christmas we moved into our new home, and after some moderate disagreement about the placement of our household decor, I did manage to keep my coffin/wine rack/bookcase out, though it was tucked into a corner of the study and not in the living room as I would have preferred and as it stands presently in my home now. And draped on top, overseeing all, was Earl The Dead Cat, complete with his very own death certificate. Earl doesn't shed much, nor go into heat, nor carouse, nor demand smelly cat food or litter boxes. He is quiet, neat and tidy, and a great conversation starter. He is even cute and cuddly in a demented sort of way.

All of this about Earl The Dead Cat reminds me of the joke about the little boy whose cat dies and the boy does not know why the cat had to die. He just does not understand and is perplexed and bewildered. After quite some time, a matter of weeks, he continues to ask his mother, "I don't understand it, I don't know why my cat has to be gone." And his mother finally says, after virtually ceaseless questioning, "Well, Dear, God took the cat because He loved your cat." The little boy pauses for a moment and then looks at his mother and says, "What does God want with a dead cat?"

## DEATH IN THE REAL WORLD

When I became a priest in 1973, I was counseling grieving survivors and conducting funeral rights for people. Largely not knowing what in blazes I was doing. I thought, "Well, this (death) will always be a relevant issue," and I've always enjoyed a challenge. So I decided to learn more. Seminary did a good job of indoctrinating me to the Episcopal Church and its customs and rites, Bible study, and theology. But it did little to equip me for the real world: counseling, parish administration, fundraising, and managing volunteers.

It turned out that my studies about death and dying had an extra benefit. Although my initial interest was in dealing with literal human death, much of my understanding of grief, bereavement, and mourning transferred to most of my counseling work as an Episcopal priest. Most of what people came to me with were other issues of loss, such as having a mastectomy, being fired, moving, confronting an empty nest, pet loss, or divorce.

In my first year out of seminary, I was the assistant in a parish and learned that loss and death come at us from many sources. One day one of our elderly members called me to say her pet dog had died. She had been widowed for years and little Fluffy was her only companion. I went to her home to console her and we did a funeral for the dog in her back yard, for which she was most appreciative. The next day my boss read me the riot act, carrying on for several minutes saying "Dogs don't have souls" and much more. I could see I would get nowhere arguing with him, so when he finally stated, "The Episcopal Church does not do dog funerals," I just looked him in the eye and said, "Now it does!" And I have been conducting pet funerals ever since.

In my second year as a priest, while I greeted parishioners as they exited the sanctuary, an elderly lady told me her pet bird had died. I expressed condolences and she went on to say, "Yes, he was the only one I had to talk to all week." That really struck me and underscored my conviction about how we underestimate the toll of pet loss, especially among the elderly.

Initially, I set out to get a degree in Thanatology, only to discover that there was no such thing in the mid 1970s. So I joined the Association for Death Education and Counseling (ADEC) in 1976, and attended many of their annual conferences and ongoing educational events. Then, since I could not get a degree in Thanatology, I decided the best way to learn about death and dying was to teach it. In 1977 I began teaching Death Education at Auburn University as an adjunct instructor through their sociology department. Sociology and Anthropology had been my college majors. Such classes are now offered through Health Care, Psychology, and other disciplines.

When I began teaching, there were only a handful of university death education courses in the country, and putting the curriculum together was a challenge. But the larger challenge was persuading Auburn University of the merits of death education. It turned out that my classes were always "sold out" with enthusiastic undergraduates. My students had a keen interest in learning about something that they knew would certainly be relevant to their lives, although most considered themselves virtually immortal at that age. The following quote by Henry Scott Holland suggests that we can look at death as nothing:

> Death is nothing at all. It does not count. I have only slipped away into the next room. Nothing has happened. Everything remains exactly as it was.

> I am I, and you are you, and the old life that we lived so fondly together is untouched, unchanged. Whatever we were to each other, that we are still. Call me by the old familiar name. Speak of me in the easy way which you always used. Put no difference into your tone. Wear no forced air of solemnity or sorrow. Laugh as we always laughed at the little jokes that we enjoyed together. Play, smile, think of me, pray for me. Let my name be ever the household word that it always was. Let it be spoken without an effort, without the ghost of a shadow upon it. Life means all that it ever meant. It is the same as it ever was. There is absolute and unbroken continuity. What is this death but a negligible accident? Why should I be out of mind because I am out of sight? I am but waiting for you, for an interval, somewhere very near, just round the corner. All is well. Nothing is hurt; nothing is lost. One brief moment and all will be as it was before. How we shall laugh at the trouble of parting when we meet again!

As we began to explore death and dying at Auburn University, I liked to use this humorous introduction to the class from a fellow death educator, Dr. Carl B. Freitag of Middle Tennessee State University:

> I'm glad we dug up enough students for this course. It's a grave responsibility: quite an undertaking to teach death and dying. Hope you didn't come in too cold. I want you to know it's not a crypt course. The text has a good plot. I'll try not to be stiff in my presentation. The course (corpse?) is well laid out and down to earth. Your grade will probably be urned. As you already know, my jokes are deadly. But the tests are murder. Some people said they wouldn't be caught dead taking this course. It is an afternoon, not a mourning class. And one of the things we'll be talking about is cremation: it's a burning issue.

While finding his remarks sufficiently disarming and amusing, I did not think his puns and witticisms would be the death of me, so I hung in there and have continued to use humor to take the edge off and open students' minds.

It was invigorating to teach death education with undergraduates who were so curious about something so alien to them. Their eyes were really opened with field trips to cemeteries, funeral homes, the morgue, etc. There was no hospice to visit at the time, as I was busy starting the first one in Alabama, but I explained the hospice concept.

We studied such topics as the way death is dealt with in various different cultures; economic aspects; death in music; the beliefs of various world religions about death; ghosts and near death experiences; the dying process; out-of-body trips and the afterlife; death in art; death in literature; the dynamics of grief, bereavement and mourning; the funeral and insurance industries (Why is it called "life insurance" rather than "death insurance?");

good versus bad deaths; preparation for death; legal aspects; one's own death; and how death was regarded and treated historically.

For example, did you know that the cross of Christian crucifixion originated with the dawn of civilization as an ancient pagan ritual designed to not offend ancient nature gods? The first humans tried to keep death at bay by elevating it on a cross to rise above their sacred earth. After hundreds of years crucifixion lost its spiritual significance and became an instrument of torture, punishment, and execution when rediscovered by Alexander the Great, who brought it back to Europe in 400 BC. Then it was reinvented again by Rome, again as torture, with suffocation occurring after several days.

In ancient Egypt, to capture and mummify dangerous animals like hundreds of crocodiles who served as messengers from this world to the next demonstrated the ancients' reverence for death. And did you know that a tribe in Africa hangs the skull of the deceased over their doorway and consults the dead regularly? From the study of death, my students and I learned a lot.

In 1990, I got my foot in the door to teach death education at the University of Arizona Medical School, but had to give up that endeavor in order to accept the leadership position of a parish in Wisconsin. Being an Episcopal Priest was still my full-time work, though I sure wish I could have educated those budding physicians about death and dying much further.

For the past four years I have offered a death education class for adults through the University of Arizona's adult education program, the Osher Lifelong Learning Institute (OLLI). We discuss everything from death-related humor to spirituality and right to die. The class is titled "Death: Certain Yet Unknown."

Of course I do not think about death and dying all the time. Nor does anyone. La Rochefoucauld commented: "One can no more look steadily at death than at the sun." At the same time we must not neglect one of the essential realities of life, in ignoring death. People tend to build up fears about topics hidden from them, and these fears grow to be worse than the realities.

Death is a biological reality, a cultural phenomenon, a spiritual event, an economic reality and a psychological process. The topic is taboo in our society, making it important to address the reality of death seriously, realistically and helpfully. We sorely need an objective and comprehensive kind of education informing our understanding of death.

> Death never comes at the right time, despite what mortals believe. Death always comes like a thief.
>
> — Christopher Pike, *The Last Vampire*

> Death, of course, should not be feared, but awaited with certain wonder. To die was to step across a threshold into a new world, unknown, unimaginable.
>
> — Juliet Marillier in *Blade of Fortriu*

## SOME DEFINITIONS

You will encounter these terms throughout this book and may want to familiarize yourself with them.

### Right to Die (RTD)

This is a moral principle based on the belief that a human being is entitled to end one's life or to undergo voluntary euthanasia.

### Physician Aid in Dying (PAD)

The phrase refers to a practice in which a physician provides a competent, terminally ill patient with a prescription for a lethal dose of medication, upon the patient's request, which the patient intends to use to end his or her own life.

### Comfort Care

Comfort care is an effort to protect or enhance quality of life without artificially prolonging life. This often includes medications such as morphine with dosages that can be increased as pain increases. Depending on the patient's situation and wishes, comfort care can also include oxygen, and perhaps stopping certain medical interventions. It may involve offering but not forcing food or fluids, keeping the patient clean, cooling or warming the patient, humidifying the room, turning lights on or off, holding the patient's hand, and comforting him/her with soothing words and music.

### Cardiopulmonary Resuscitation (CPR)

This was developed to assist victims facing imminent sudden death from causes such as heart attack or trauma, and increases the likelihood of long-term survival. Unless a doctor or other licensed health-care provider authorizes a Do Not Resuscitate (DNR) or you have a valid Prehospital Medical Care Directive, CPR is administered virtually every time a person's heart stops. Talk to your doctor to learn more about why you might choose to accept or reject CPR, and the methods of CPR you want or do not want.

### Artificially Administered Food and Fluids

These can be administered by medical procedures, including intravenous treatment or by various types of tubes inserted into the body. (If food and fluid can be taken by spoon, drink, or other natural means, it is not artificially administered.)

### Autopsy

While state laws differ, in general an autopsy may be required when a person dies who was not under the current care of a physician for a potentially fatal illness, and/or the physician is unavailable or unwilling to sign a death certificate. This might happen if a person dies at home. However, if the person's doctor is willing to sign a death certificate or if the person is under the care of a hospice and its physician will sign the death certificate, an autopsy will probably not be required. In some cases, a dying patient or family members may voluntarily request an autopsy to determine more accurately the medical condition that caused death. There is usually a charge for a voluntary autopsy.

### Do Not Resuscitate (DNR) or Allow Natural Death (AND)

This might also be referred to as a pre-hospital medical directive. This document is signed by you and your doctor that informs emergency medical technicians (EMTs) or hospital emergency personnel not to resuscitate you. EMTs and other emergency personnel will not use equipment, drugs, or devices to restart your heart or breathing, but they will not withhold medical interventions that are necessary to provide comfort care or to alleviate pain.

Important Note: Depending on your state's laws or regulations, there may be a number of specific requirements. For example, in my home state of Arizona, a Prehospital Medical Care Directive or DNR must be on letter-sized paper or wallet-sized paper on an orange background to be valid. You can either attach a picture to this form, or complete the personal information. You must also complete the form and sign it in front of a witness. Your health care provider and your witness must sign this.

### Durable Medical Health Care Power of Attorney (POA)

This is an essential document that names someone that you trust to act as your agent if you are unable to speak for yourself, or perhaps sooner. If you want to choose one person to speak for you on health care matters, and someone else to make financial decisions, you can do separate financial and health care powers of attorney.

### Life Support

This a generic term for measures to keep you alive, including food and/or fluids (nutrition/hydration); cardiopulmonary resuscitation (CPR) by equipment, devices, or drugs; and breathing devices such as a ventilator. Under what circumstances do you want some, all, or no life support to be administered? To be withheld? To be removed or stopped? Why and which ones? What about withholding or withdrawing life-sustaining treatment if you are known to be pregnant and there is the possibility that with treatment the embryo/fetus will develop to the point of a live birth? What about medical care necessary to treat your condition until your doctors reasonably conclude that your condition is terminal or is irreversible and incurable or you are in a persistent vegetative state?

### Living Will

This is the most common form of an Advance Directive and it spells out your preferences about certain kinds of life-sustaining treatments. For example, you can indicate whether you do or do not want interventions such as cardiac resuscitation, tube feeding, and mechanical respiration.

### Organ and Body Donation

You can determine if you want to donate organs or tissues, and if you do, then what organs or tissues do you want to donate, for what purposes, and to what organizations. An alternative is to donate your body to a medical school. You may make such arrangements or you can leave the choice to your representative.

### Variations in State Law

Even though all states have laws for "advance directives" or Life Care Planning, the laws may be somewhat different. Normally the law of the state where treatment occurs controls, not the law of the state where medical forms were signed. If you spend time in more than one state and reasonably conclude you may need medical treatment in more than one state, you might want to have your forms comply with the laws of the states where you might be treated, to the extent possible.

# 1 What Is a Good Death?

*As one wag exclaimed: "The best death is one that happens to someone else!"*

*Another: "I am not afraid of dying, But I am terribly unhappy about not living."*

Different people have different concepts of what makes for a good death, though there do seem to be some rather universal factors that are commonly considered. I first began to learn about how to enable a good death through my work with hospices in the mid 1970s. I first spoke publicly about a good death about 18 years ago, and although my views have evolved a bit since then, fundamentally they have not changed much.

How might we die well? Modern American society — unlike other cultures and times — has no standard, no widely held concept of what constitutes a noble death, a virtuous death, a dignified death and therefore a good death. This has not always been true. Others have had the jousting knight in shining armor, the samurai, the wise and revered elder, or some form of a socially acceptable or noble death. I am writing here about some aspects of goodness at the time of death, rather than "death with dignity" (a political movement to support aid in dying). I'm not sure there really can be a truly dignified death, or an entirely good death. After all, who wants to die? Who wants a loved one to die? Nevertheless, it will happen.

We need a new approach to death. When death is viewed as a failure rather than as an important part of life, individuals are diverted from preparing for it, and medicine falls short in helping people die a good death. We need a new approach to death. It is time to break the taboo around death and take back control of a subject that has been medicalized, professionalized, and sanitized to such an extent that it is now alien to most Americans' daily lives.

One of the first books published in 1474 by William Caxton, England's first printer, was a manual of how to die. It remained a bestseller for two centuries. It was not until after the Reformation that European death became macabre, and Francis Bacon was the first to suggest that doctors might hold death at bay. Earlier Arab and Jewish doctors had thought it blasphemous for doctors to attempt to interfere with death. For Paracelsus, death was "a return to the womb."

What we are addicted to now, it seems, is the belief that we can micromanage death. We tend to think of a good death as one that we can control, making decisions about how much intervention, how much pain relief, whether our final moments are in the home or the hospital, who will be by our side. We even sometimes try to make decisions about what we will die from. This can be valuable, as when a cancer patient with little hope of survival rejects debilitating chemotherapy. But often, our best-laid plans go awry. Dying is awfully hard to choreograph. Caitlin Doughty, a mortician who advocates acceptance of death, writes:

> For me, the good death includes being prepared to die, with my affairs in order, the good and bad messages delivered that need delivering. The good death means dying while I still have my mind sharp and aware; it also means dying without having to endure large amounts of suffering and pain. The good death means accepting death as inevitable, and not fighting it when the time comes. This is my good death, but as legendary psychotherapist Carl Jung said, "It won't help to hear what I think about death. Your relationship to mortality is your own."

R. Alan Woods, in *The Journey Is The Destination: A Photo Journal,* says "we die well when we die with purpose fulfilled." And there is an old Sufi saying, "the happiness of the drop is to die in the river."

## The Death I Would Like

My concept of a good death might also be called "the least worst death." As an Episcopal priest for over forty years, I have seen all manner of death. Most of those I have witnessed were horrible: full of pain and suffering, lacking love and support, and not at all the way the dying person wanted to die.

As I ponder this concept of a least-worst death, my notions include some of the following: it would be good not to die alone, to have the companionship of my family and others whom I love and who love me. It would be good to be free from physical pain, and to be free from the fear of recurring pain. The anxiety and dread that physical pain may return can be as disabling as the pain itself. And it would be good to receive treatment that reflects and honors my wishes.

I would like to be in friendly, familiar surroundings — preferably at home, with my own belongings, in my own place. That may mean having my favorite pictures on the wall, my pet dog by my side, and the accustomed view out the window. In other words, it would be good to be in control as much as possible: to make decisions regarding my care, and to have those decisions honored. It would be good to be touched, to be held, or to be left alone, as I may need. And I hope to be free to express my emotions — to be angry, to cry, to retain a sense of humor, to laugh, to love.

It would also be good if those around me could express what they feel. Sometimes people tip-toe too much around the dying person. I would prefer straightforward talk, including knowing the truth, even painful truth. Too often the truth is withheld from the dying person.

Of course, I do not want to be financially exploited. I want to know my insurance coverage and have financial affairs in order. During the last six months of life, the average American is encumbered with over half of all lifetime medical expenses. And the funeral industry maintains subtle practices of financial exploitation. I think my plans will prevent this from happening.

I hope to have led a purposeful life and to be able to have that life affirmed before I die. I'd like to reflect with others on that life: successes, flaws and all. This book itself and my campaigning for the right to die well has been a large part of my purpose for the past two decades.

Another aspiration I have is to be free from emotional pain and to be at peace with myself. This may include having taken care of literal and figurative unfinished business — having made funeral plans, body donation plans, setting monetary plans in order, updating my will, being at peace with my God and dying with a kind heart, and so on. And it may include having made an effort to reconcile former interpersonal conflicts, to put relationships straight (including saying goodbye). It would be good to die knowing that my family will receive emotional help with bereavement.

I close these personal reflections with the hope and conviction that we can all do more to enable a better death, the least-worst death. Your loved one's death may be greatly soothed by the munificence of your putting this knowledge to work on their behalf.

## CHANGE IS NEEDED

Specialized care is needed when a person is near death. Physical and mental changes occur that can confuse and frighten those around them and result in inappropriate responses. When one can no longer take food orally, the temptation is to use a feeding tube. When a dying person gasps for air, the tendency is to reach for an oxygen mask. But are these desirable? Not necessarily, experts say. In fact, such interventions can do more harm than good.

Our death-denying culture has led to a system of care for the terminally ill that allows us to indulge the fantasy that dying is somehow optional. In many ways, we act as if we can avoid death indefinitely if only we are quick enough or smart enough or prepared enough. Even hospice workers call their field by a new name that accentuates the positive: they used to say they specialized in "death and dying," but today the umbrella term is "end of life." The shift is subtle but significant — an emphasis on "life" rather than "death." What we have, then, is a medical system for the dying that is as ambivalent about dying as we are ourselves.

That is not surprising. Who can say what it is really like to die? You get only one chance to do it, and there is no reporting back from the field. In her book *Handbook for Mortals*, written with Joan Harrold, Joanne Lynn, who is also a senior scientist at the RAND Corporation, wrote about a seriously ill patient who opens his eyes and sees a nurse. "Am I dead yet?" he asks. "No," says the nurse. He thinks for a moment and then asks, "How will I know?"

When it comes to self-imposed death, to help us out of the maze of terminology and distinctions, the Protestant moralist Robert Paul Ramsay has suggested the alternative term *agathanasia*, which I rather like. Combining the Greek adjective *agathos*, meaning good, and the noun *thanatos*, meaning death, this new term is free of the emotional connotations that euthanasia stirs up and that often preclude intelligent discussion of the issue. And many misinterpret euthanasia as someone acting upon someone else. Ramsay uses this term to refer to a death with dignity. Many moralists, like Curran, Ramsay, and Haring, while they would condemn positive euthanasia and advocate an ethics of agathanasia, would share with others the concern for the values of compassion and human freedom.

## Insights of Others

The Greek philosopher Epicuris said "The art of living well and dying well are one." Dame Cicely Mary Saunders was an English Anglican nurse, social worker, physician and writer, involved with many international universities. She is best known for her role in the birth of the modern hospice movement, emphasizing the importance of palliative care in modern medicine. Says she: "How people die remains in the memories of those who live on."

And remember the words of Ralph Waldo Emerson: "It is one of the most beautiful compensations in life that no man can sincerely try to help another without helping himself."

In *Love in the Time of Cholera*, Gabriel García Márquez writes, "Each man is master of his own death and all that we can do when the time comes is to help him die without fear of pain." And in his book *Lies My Teacher Told Me*, James W. Loewen reports:

> Many African societies divide humans into three categories: those still alive on the earth, the sasha, and the zamani. The recently departed whose time on earth overlapped with people still here are the sasha, the living-dead. They are not wholly dead, for they still live in the memories of the living, who can call them to mind, create their likeness in art, and bring them to life in anecdote. When the last person to know an ancestor dies,

> that ancestor leaves the sasha for the zamani, the dead. As generalized ancestors, the zamani are not forgotten but revered. Many can be recalled by name. But they are not the living-dead. There is a difference.

A few other relevant quotations expressing thoughts on the quality of death:

> Memories are of the ethereal, and not the material world, that is how I know I am forever.
>
> — Michael Poeltl

> I mean, they say you die twice. One time when you stop breathing and a second time, a bit later on, when somebody says your name for the last time.
>
> — Banksy

> Carve your name on hearts, not tombstones. A legacy is etched into the minds of others and the stories they share about you.
>
> — Shannon L. Alder

> More are men's ends marked than their lives before. The setting sun, the music at the close, as the last taste of sweets, is sweetest last, writ in remembrance more than things long past.
>
> — William Shakespeare, *Richard II*

Some research about what constitutes a good death can be found in Appendix K.

Poets, professors, priests, and plain folks all opine about what makes a "good death." In truth, deaths are nearly as unique as the lives that came before them: shaped by the attitudes, physical conditions, medical treatments, and mix of people that accompany them. You, and only you, can determine what your good death may be. How would you like to die?

# Saying Goodbye
## Communicating at the End of Life

## 2

*A dying man needs to die, as a sleepy man needs to sleep, and there comes a time when it is wrong, as well as useless, to resist.*

— Stewart Alsop

There are a number of practical considerations to take into account when someone you love is approaching death. These include what to do and what not to do when interacting with a dying person.

Far too many people in our culture do not know how to talk about death. Throughout much of life, this may not pose a problem. But what happens when someone we love is dying of a terminal illness? If we have never had any practice talking about death, will we be able to say what we mean when it really counts?

> Death. It's around more than people realize. Because no one wants to talk about it or hear about it. It's too sad. Too painful. Too hard. The list of reasons is endless.
>
> — Jessica Sorensen, *Nova and Quinton: No Regrets*

The Conversation Project (*theconversationproject.org*), dedicated to helping people talk about their wishes for end-of-life care, offers this perspective:

> Too many people are dying in a way they wouldn't choose, and too many of their loved ones are left feeling bereaved, guilty, and uncertain. It's time to transform our culture so we shift from not talking about dying to talking about it. It's time to share the way we want to live at the end of our lives. And it's time to communicate about the kind of care we want and don't want for ourselves. We believe that the place for this to begin is at the kitchen table — not in the intensive care unit — with the people we love, before it's too late. Together we can make these difficult conversations easier. We can make sure that our own wishes and those of our loved ones are expressed and respected. If you're ready to join us, we ask you: Have you had the conversation?

According to the National Hospice Foundation, one-quarter of American adults over age forty-five say they would be unwilling to talk to their parents about their parents' death, even if their parents had been told they had less than six months to live. Half of all Americans said they were counting on friends and family members to carry out their wishes about how they wanted to die, yet seventy-five percent of them had never spelled out those wishes to anyone. A significant subset of that seventy-five percent had probably never even articulated their wishes to themselves.

The first thing to remember is that the process of dying is basically a process of grieving. Little by little, the terminally ill person is facing loss of everyone and everything. First, there are small physical losses, the loss of the ability to take long walks, for example. Gradually these losses become more difficult to cope with. Along with physical losses, the individual must begin to face other kinds of loss, such as the loss of a future spent with a spouse, or children and grandchildren. The realization by the ill person that he or she is dying becomes a part of everything felt and thought.

As in all communication, our tasks are to listen closely, and to speak openly and honestly. Beyond this, when communicating at the end of life, we must use sensitivity and our knowledge of the unique situation. For example, a person who is "bargaining" (i.e., the state in which the ill person tries to bargain with doctors, family, clergy, or God to "buy more time") probably does not want to hear that funeral plans must be made immediately because time is running out. Likewise, a person who is very angry may not respond well to a heart-to-heart talk about finding positive meaning in terminal illness.

On the other hand, most of us err too much on the side of caution with painful topics. It is false to assume that most terminally ill people do not know they are dying. Most know it full well: just as Elizabeth "Beth" March explained on her deathbed to her dear sister Josephine "Jo" March in *Little Women*, "I am not afraid. I can be brave like you. But I know I shall be homesick for you, even in Heaven."

You might ask something like "How serious do you think your situation is?" Or "What is your understanding of where things stand now with your illness?" Often one will respond by acknowledging that death is on the horizon. In addition, it is wrong to assume that their willingness to talk about their condition is diminished. If anything, this may be a contemplative time of life for many people. Religious faith and interest in the spiritual side of life may grow, as may the need to reflect upon one's past and one's relationships.

## Spirituality, Religion, the Soul

Let me digress a bit here to address the topics of religious interest and spiritual awareness. I regard spirituality as the essence of what makes humans different from animals: the existence of a "soul." The spirit is the innermost being of an individual in relationship to and with God, self, other humans, and the environment. Spirituality includes such concepts as the meaning and purpose of life, transcendence, connectedness, love, caring, and hope.

Attendance and participation in mainstream religious organizations is declining. A poll conducted in 2013 asked 80,000 people in various denominations about their spiritual aspirations, and it revealed gaps between aspects of church life that members see as important to their spiritual growth and how those needs are being met by their local church. The three biggest gaps were the following:

1. Help me understand the Bible in depth (25%)
2. Help me in time of emotional need (28%)
3. Help me to develop relationships that encourage accountability (28%)

In others words, these are the chief ways in which parishioners feel that their church has let them down in their spiritual journeys. The bottom line is that what people want is often not what the church is giving them.

I consider the following to be core spiritual tools:

- Forgiveness: letting go of your hurt and the hurt of others.
- Gratitude: appreciating everything and everyone in your world.
- Love: giving without expecting to receive.
- Prayer: direct communication with God or the divine.
- Meditation: visiting your inner space and centering yourself. Also called "mindfulness."

I rather like the following alphabetical list from the Dalai Lama, which I think touches on the key elements of leading a spiritually fulfilling life:

## LIVE ONE DAY AT A TIME AND MAKE IT A MASTERPIECE

**A** void negative sources, people, places & habits
**B** elieve in yourself
**C** onsider things from every angle
**D** on't give up and don't give in
**E** verything you're looking for lies behind the mask you wear
**F** amily & friends are hidden treasures, seek them & enjoy their riches
**G** ive more than you planned to

**H** ang on to your dreams
**I** f opportunity doesn't knock, build a door
**J** udge your success by what you had to give up in order to get it
**K** eep trying no matter how hard it seems
**L** ove yourself
**M** ake it happen
**N** ever lie, cheat or steal
**O** pen your arms to change, but don't let go of your values
**P** ractice makes perfect
**Q** uality not quantity in anything you do
**R** emember that silence is sometimes the best answer
**S** top procrastinating
**T** ake control of your own destiny
**U** nderstand yourself in order to better understand others
**V** isualize it
**W** hen you lose, don't lose the lesson
**X** cellence in all your efforts
**Y** ou are unique, nothing can replace you
**Z** ero in on your target and go for it

## Afterlife And Fear of Death

And then there is the issue of life after death. All major religions provide some notion of a continuance beyond our bodily existence. Some people take this quite seriously, while others do not, such as Woody Allen proclaiming "I don't want to attain immortality through my work. I want to attain immortality by not dying." I believe that death is and shall remain a mystery. Why speculate about what cannot be known?

There is a story told by oral tradition, wherein a Jew asks a fourth-century rabbi to show himself in a dream after he has died. Upon showing himself, the man asks the rabbi if death was painful. The rabbi replies that death was as painless as lifting a hair from a cup of milk and adds that if God were to tell the rabbi that he may return to his life he would not chose to do so because the fear of death would be too great.

Here are a few more commentaries about fear of death:

> There is a thin line that separates life from death, but once it's crossed, it becomes as large as an ocean, and so treacherous that it's impossible to cross back.
>
> — Federico Chini, *The Sea Of Forgotten Memories*

> To fear death, gentlemen, is no other than to think oneself wise when one is not, to think one knows what one does not know. No one knows whether death may not be the greatest of all blessings for a man, yet men fear it as if they knew that it is the greatest of evils.
>
> — Socrates

> Fear of death is irrational. We all know we will die one day. But again we are irrational beings.
>
> — Bangambiki Habyarimana, *The Great Pearl of Wisdom*

> I am young now and can look upon my body and soul with pride. But it will be mangled soon, and later it will begin to disintegrate, and then I shall die, and die conclusively. How can we face such a fact, and not live in fear?
>
> — Jack Kerouac

> There was no hope in death, only an end.
>
> — Morgan Rhodes, *Rebel Spring*

> I've been to the other side.... You're dead there, too.
>
> — Courtney Kirchoff, *Jaden Baker*

> How nice — to feel nothing, and still get full credit for being alive.
>
> — Kurt Vonnegut, *Slaughterhouse-Five*

> We choose our next world through what we learn in this one. Learn nothing, and the next world is the same as this one, all the same limitations and lead weights to overcome.
>
> — Richard Bach, *Jonathan Livingston Seagull*

Sigmund Freud, who believed that the afterlife is "mere illusion," stated that the whole idea of immortality is a sign of despair and limitation, invented to compensate for the misery of our life on earth. In reality, he claimed, death is annihilation, a return to "inorganic lifelessness."

As a priest I would sometimes be asked about my views on the afterlife, to which I would usually reply something like, "What I believe is not as important as what you believe. What are your thoughts? If your belief works for you, that is what counts." Sometimes I would be a bit more cynical, speculating that I wonder if some people even have a life after birth, let alone after death. You have heard the expression: "Get a life!" which is often said to express disapproval or disdain. And I might allude to my bumper sticker that reads "I believe in life BEFORE death."

Did you know that it seems single celled organisms are immortal? I don't fully understand this, but you can look it up on the Internet.

## Balancing Beliefs

I have used the following as a balance sheet to help people examine their beliefs about what awaits us after death: the assets and liabilities of belief in an afterlife.

### Assets

A1) It provides hope at the point of death and a way to cope with our deaths. As Francois de la Rochefoucauld commented, "However difficult hope may be, yet she carries us on pleasantly to the end of life."

A2) It infuses life with a sense of meaning and purpose if the afterlife is seen as a reward for a good life.

A3) It gives us a reason to be moral and a way to transmit morality to our children.

A4) Clinical evidence shows that religious people who affirm the afterlife are healthier than those who do not.

### Liabilities

L1) You may not take action to seek justice in this life if you assume it will be provided in the next.

L2) You may live in constant fear that any sin you might have committed will condemn you to an eternity of suffering in Hell.

L3) You may not exercise your own best judgment in matters and allow yourself to be controlled by others who claim sacred authority.

L4) You may not live your life to the fullest if you think that it is not the only life you have.

While I would never argue against contrary beliefs held by a dying person, I personally do not believe that anyone has died and returned to life. Death is final, permanent, and absolute. Nor do I believe in communication with the dead via channeling any more than I believe some people have fatidic powers. There is a Sufi saying: "I heard a voice whispering to me in the night. It said there is no such thing as a voice whispering in the night."

When I taught death education to undergraduates at Auburn University, we studied out-of-body trips, near-death experiences, ghosts, and the like. Who knows? Perhaps in the future humans will evolve to communicating with those who have predeceased us, but not now.

## THE VALUE OF HUMOR

A dying person is not a china doll. Chances are, he or she would like to be approached in an honest manner, even if it means working through old disappointments or hurts. In fact, many dying people welcome this time as an opportunity to "clear the air" with family members. And remember, dying people still almost always have a sense of humor, and the same emotions as the rest of us. In conversations with them, it is okay to tell jokes. To deny laughter to those who are anticipating or near death is to deny humor as a part of life. To lose humor is to lose life.

Early in the book *One Flew Over The Cuckoo's Nest*, Randle Patrick McMurphy makes a tremendously insightful observation when he enters the insane asylum: "The first thing that got me about this place — there wasn't anybody laughing. I haven't heard a real laugh since I came through that door. Man, when you lose your laugh, you lose your footing."

In 1975, I had the privilege of attending the world premiere of the film version of *One Flew Over The Cuckoo's Nest* at the Kennedy Center in Washington, DC. It was a great movie, but, at times, a little too close to home for comfort, as I had just worked for three months in a state mental hospital that could have come right out of that movie — it was scary. But we had a wonderful time at the premiere. We had dined with Jack Nicholson, Danny DeVito, Louise Fletcher (Nurse Ratched), Michael Douglas, and the whole cast. The movie went on to win five Oscars that year, including best picture. But none of that impressed me more than Randle Patrick McMurphy's observation about laughter.

The movie premiere was a fundraiser for Inter/Met Seminary, an interfaith theological school conceived and directed by the Rev. John Fletcher, a personal friend of mine and brother of Louise, the actress. Inter/Met was a wonderful school that unfortunately survived only a few years, but stressed important new concepts for pastoral ministry. (More about Inter/Met can be found in Appendix J.)

It is my conviction that life no more ceases to be humorous in the face of death than it ceases to be serious in the face of laughter. There is usually no need to tip-toe around the dying person.

I remember attending a conference of the Association for Death Education and Counseling in Philadelphia in the early 1980s. The most heavily attended workshops were those relating to humor, which reinforced my view that a bit of humorous relief and release can go a long way in balancing our serious thoughts, feelings, and experiences when working with death and dying. Because humor helps to lighten up such weighty matters, we have to be able to laugh, to tell tales about the lighter side of life, to take the edge off, to unwind.

A fellow priest tells me he once took the edge off for himself when, at the internment following the funeral ceremony, instead of saying, "In the name of the Father, and of the Son, and of the Holy Ghost" he uttered this mondegeen: "In the name of the Father, and of the Son, and in the hole he goes."

Many years ago I attended a state hospice convention in Michigan. Attendees were seated for the dinner banquet, with eight of us at each of about twenty round tables. At my behest, our table rather spontaneously composed a limerick and read it to all. Before we knew it, people at each table proceeded to create their own funny poem, each group trying to generate more laughter than the other. It really lifted the weight off of the heavy subject.

Humor is a safety valve for the discharge of tense emotion. In cutting through the discomforting experience, humor may purge us. At a funeral at which I presided, the surviving members of the family were seated up front together, but there was some confusion as to who would be sitting where. They changed seats a couple of times and someone in the group remarked, "Gee, here it is a funeral and we're playing musical chairs!" The comment didn't engender raucous laughter, but it served to break the tension with smiles.

## Communicating with a Dying Person: Dos and Don'ts

While it is best to let the dying person take the lead in communicating, this is not always simple. While listening for verbal cues and being sensitive, also balance this caution with your own need for self-expression. Every situation is a little different. Honesty is the best policy, but we also need a starting point. The following are some dos and don'ts for honest conversation with a person at the end of life.

### Do

Do ask the dying person if he or she wants to talk. Assess the person's comfort level with the topic of death and dying. Do not make any assumptions.

Do think ahead of time about what you want to say and how you want to say it. Would you rather open up conversation and see what happens, or do you have specific things you would like to express? Is it a simple goodbye? Do you have something you have always been grateful for, or something for which you would like to apologize?

Do think about the setting of your discussion. Would you like a chance to be alone with your loved one, or are there important discussions to have as a family?

Do think of alternative ways of communication. Are you more comfortable with written communication? Then maybe you could write the dying person a letter. If you are too uncomfortable to communicate verbally, are there nonverbal ways you'd like to express your love and appreciation? For example, homemade photo albums or special mementos that are significant to the dying person. An even easier approach may be to forget words entirely, and do something for or with the patient that expresses how you feel. Turn on a ball game; listen to a favorite piece of music; read some old letters; sit on the porch and watch the rain; flip through a scrapbook.

Do say it even if they can't hear you. What if the patient cannot communicate? Should you still have a farewell if it is only one-way? I say emphatically, "Yes"!

Do remember that many ill persons feel guilty for leaving us, and may worry about our feelings more than their own. If you can, help them understand that while things will change in their absence, life will go on, and that you will be okay. It may be helpful to give the person "permission" to die. "It's OK to let go."

Do go to "Plan B" if you are dealing with the rare person who declines to talk at all, and you still have the need to acknowledge the situation. Talk with others: friends and family. It helps to get your message down to the absolute essentials. What is the very most important thing you want that person to know? You also may need to accept that you will not get to say what you wanted.

## Don't

Don't try to force the dying person to express his/her feelings within your time frame. Be patient.

Don't nag your loved one to talk more than he/she is comfortable. Denial is a normal way of coping with overwhelming information and emotion. Some people never move beyond the wish to simply ignore the illness. This wish can be respected to the extent possible.

Don't express discomfort when the bereaved person is angry, fearful, or depressed.

Don't avoid important topics for fear of "upsetting" the dying person. It can be more upsetting to have loved ones ignore obvious realities!

Don't assume that because you encounter death or illness in your job (e.g., medical personnel, police and fire personnel, or insurance professionals) you will know just what to say. All bets are off when it comes to your own family member or friend. Take off your professional hat and say what is in your heart.

Don't take outbursts of anger personally. These may be a normal occurrence within the dying process.

Don't assume that positive emotions are the only kind of emotion allowed. For some, illness can last for some time. Many people report having a chance to work through old wounds and misunderstandings during the end-of-life process. It is okay to feel more than one feeling at once, and to express more than one kind of emotion.

As you can see, there are few guidelines for how to say goodbye. Having a chance to say goodbye at all is a precious gift. A simple, "I've always loved you" or "You were the best father I could have asked for" can go a long way toward easing your grief after the death. In addition, it is important to the dying person. Reassuring words from loved ones can help a dying person to let go, knowing that everything that needed to be said was said.

Again, you might also give permission to die, letting the dying person know that although you will miss them, and there will be a void in their absence, you will manage. In his book *Without You*, the actor Anthony Rapp retells a story from his mother's days as a pediatric nurse:

> "There was this little boy I was taking care of," she said, "and he was terminally ill, and we all knew it, but he kept hanging on and hanging on. He wouldn't die, it was so sad. And his parents were always there with him, giving him so much love and support, but he was in so much pain, and it really was time for him to go. So finally some of us nurses took his father aside and we told him, 'You have to tell your son it's okay for him to go. You have to give him permission.' And so the father took his son in his arms and he sat with him in a chair and held on to him and told him over and over, that it was okay for him to go, and, well, after a few moments, his son died."

# Why I and Some of My Colleagues Became Involved in Advocating Death with Dignity

# 3

*Dying on your own terms, this is the greatest gift anyone can bestow upon a mortal man.*
— Mario Stinger, *Destined for Oblivion: As Nature Intended*

IN THE U.S., THE RIGHT to die is increasingly accepted yet remains controversial. Seeking the help of a physician to choose the timing of one's death is explicitly allowed in only a handful of states, although several other states are weighing it. Whenever legislation on this subject is considered, public hearings draw countless opponents, whose objections are usually on religious grounds.

If you are already committed to the right of a person to make choices about leaving this planet in a dignified way, you may want to just browse over this chapter. But for anybody still thinking through the moral issues, it may be helpful to understand why some of us have become passionate on the subject.

Over the past twenty years, I have worked closely with many passionate people who support and advocate for the right to die: for the right to choose one's own death and to accomplish it with dignity. Coming from various backgrounds and experiences, they have all arrived at the same conclusion that each person deserves to have freedom of choice in dying, just as we exercise choices in how we live. I asked several people who have worked with me over the years in the right to die movement to explain why they became involved, and their responses are below. Last names are omitted in the interest of privacy.

## Karen T.

Call it a strong sense of my civil rights that brought me to join Choices Arizona. I've always loved that phrase, "All laws stop at the tip of my nose," and that includes my right to see to my own death if I choose to die with dignity.

## John T.

Why I came to EOLC (End Of Life Choices): like any good American, I grew up unaware of dying and death. These concepts were not part of public consciousness and were not even really allowable in "polite" conversation. According to popular American culture, the point of living is to be forever young, which automatically means that dying is not an option. Dying and death are not part of one's life plan; getting old and dying is certainly not part of the American dream. In fact, dying and death are not acceptable, are seen as somehow un-American, and should be made illegal if not already illegal. Perhaps an amendment to the Constitution could be passed to ban it, and the Department of Homeland Security wouldn't issue Death an entry visa (would Death want a tourist or business visa?). That would prevent Death from entering our land and condemn it to obscurity and impotence.

But experience, the best teacher in life, taught me that death could not be banished. A major injury years ago put me in great pain and made me realize that I would not want to continue living my life if that kind of pain were the price. Fortunately an operation put me back on the path of living well. A few years later, my mother died, peacefully at home in no pain, cared for by her daughter, who was also a registered nurse. I learned to be grateful for my mother's peaceful death and pondered my own. That led me to do volunteer work for a hospice, visiting dying patients.

My first and most memorable assignment was with a professional truck driver. Dying caught him on the freeway as he was driving his truck across the country and let him linger in a hospice in Denver until the end. He was miserable, angry, harsh, ungrateful, and in denial. He was also in pain and literally without a relative or friend in the world.

Because he was indigent and friendless, his facility and care were substandard, far below what I would ever want for myself. The dollar speaks, even in dying. I sneaked him cigarettes, his one pleasure, for which he never thanked me. It was unpleasant visiting this lost soul, and he died a lonely and very sad death, with virtually no control over any aspect of leaving this world. Again, I learned about dying and death, but this time from the opposite side of the spectrum from my mother's peaceful death.

The cumulative effect of these and other experiences illuminated and reinforced my hope to have a death I could look back on with satisfaction. Above all, I realized I wanted to die pain-free and with as much control as I could. I have always tried to live an 'examined' life, seeking to make the best choices consciously and in harmony with my principles. To have control over my dying process and death is just a continuation of how I have always lived. It is simply the last decision in the living process, and we all should have the right to create and direct the last act. End of Life Choices supports this basic right and works to create the conditions that allow for dying with dignity. For this reason, I support EOLC's mission and work.

### VICKY F.

I have been volunteering for all my adult life. One of my proudest possessions is the Margaret Sanger award given to me March 18, 1974 for "recognition of significant contributions to family planning." I believed wholeheartedly in their concept that every child should be a wanted child and a woman should be able to control her body.

In 1989, I took an extensive hospice training course. When we moved to Green Valley, Arizona, I decided that my volunteering days were over. I wanted to take some courses at the U. of A., go to the movies, read, and play lots of golf. Then, in March 1993, I picked up the *Arizona Daily Star* and on the front page was an article about a police officer who went out on a street corner and shot himself in the head with his service revolver. The police officer and his wife were old and ill. They wanted to die together. They did not want one to be left alone. They checked into a motel, took their pills, and said their goodbyes.

But that afternoon when the maid came in she found the woman dead, but the man was still alive. Of course they rushed him to the hospital and resuscitated him. That was why he went to a street corner and shot himself in the head!

At the end of the article they mentioned the Hemlock Society and Dr. John Westover. I, who was never going to volunteer again, picked up the Tucson phone book and called John Westover. I asked, "I don't know anything about this Hemlock Society, could you send me some information?" Within three months I was on the board, became treasurer and then president. At that time, 1994, there were only two chapters in Arizona: Tucson and Phoenix.

John Westover, Jean Chitlener, Bud Whichenlow, John Abraham, myself, and probably others that I can't recall right now, drove up and down Arizona and opened eight new chapters. When my dear Ed became ill, I had to resign as the Tucson Chapter President, but later I became president of the Green Valley Chapter. Then became a state board member and then president of the state organization, Arizonans for Death and Dignity.

I felt strongly about a woman's right to choose and I feel just as strongly about a terminal competent person's rights to choose when to end their suffering. I only hope I live long enough to see a law that makes it legal for a suffering, competent person to quietly, calmly, and with dignity, end an existence that has no joy, satisfaction, or happiness.

## VJ P.

As a young dancer, I watched older dancers suffer because they hadn't planned well. Their embarrassment was almost contagious. I promised myself that I would bow out gracefully. I specifically promised myself that I would leave show business when I began to appear to be 30 years old. Dancers, similar to athletes, are considered to be "over the hill" once they are about 30 years old.

Little did I realize what a valuable lesson I was cultivating — one of the very few important lessons I was able to learn from others rather than having to experience the agony of the lesson myself. Little did I realize how well I would be able to apply the principle of "bowing out gracefully" to other activities in my life.

At the age of 32, I unexpectedly looked into a mirror and saw the 30-year-old-looking woman I had been waiting to see. I gave myself one year to find another occupation. One year later, to the day, I raised my hand and was sworn in to the Woman's Army Corps. I changed costumes.

A few years before the 20-year anniversary of my military service, I analyzed the pros and cons of continuing my military service beyond 20 years. As an older female in a male-dominated institution, I decided, again to "bow out gracefully." I was tired of over-compensating. Whether or not I could continue to prove that I was physically fit became less important than whether or not I wanted to continue to prove that I was physically fit. "Bowing out gracefully" was an easier decision than it had been as a dancer.

The ethical stance of the Hemlock philosophy is compatible with my personal life stance. Quality of life is most important to me. An afterlife is not one of my concerns: When the lights go out, the lights simply go out. I had no choice about how I entered life. I do have some choice in how I exit life. More than anything, though, I hope that I have the courage, foresight, and sense of timing to bow out gracefully.

## Jean O.

As volunteer communications director for End of Life Choices Arizona, I take this opportunity to relate two stories about why I got involved in the death with dignity movement. Stories about two wonderful, loving, caring people very close to me who died with anything but dignity. With their bodies full of cancer, they could not be completely anesthetized with any of the palliative care they received at the end of their lives.

My mother was diagnosed with pancreatic cancer in December 1993 and died in April 1994. Hospice nurses came to our home to administer palliative care only in the last few weeks of her existence and, since they were unable to be there on a 24-hour-a-day schedule, there were many times when Mother would cry out in pain and there was nothing I could do for her. I was unable to administer drugs intravenously to relieve her suffering and she was unable to swallow the potent liquid prescription. She slipped into a coma and had to be taken by ambulance back to the hospital. She died approximately five hours later.

The second agonizing death I witnessed was my significant other of 21 years. He was a retired Air Force General and fighter pilot, who had proudly served his country for thirty years. In 1989, he had to have his cancerous vocal chords removed. For almost nine years he lived a reasonably happy life and used the voice box apparatus designed for laryngectomy patients. In 1998, his cancer returned and ruthlessly spread throughout his body. In the end, he was unable to communicate due to the fact that he could no longer hold the voice box to his throat and that device was his only contact with the world. Because of his special breathing needs, I was unable to care for him at home, and once again I was a helpless observer of an excruciating imminent death. This lugubrious event lasted for ten months and ended by withdrawal of all tubes connected to his fragile body.

As these two loved ones were perishing, I made a tacit promise to them that I would do everything in my power to change the way terminally ill humans are treated. I believe working with the End of Life Choices organization is a good start.

## Renée N.

From 1974 to 1976 I lost three grandparents and a father-in-law. One died in the arms of his daughter, but another died alone in the hospital, both after suffering with cancer for years. The other two died in their sleep after short illnesses. So it was a marked contrast in how they died, and I knew I'd never want to suffer for a long time as two of my loved ones had.

In 1976, I saw the film *Robin and Marian* in which a seriously wounded, older Robin Hood is given a deadly poison by Maid Marian, who knows he will never recover from his wounds. She also imbibes the poison herself, choosing not to live without the love of her life. Her statement "I love you more than God" made a profound impression on me. By my twenties, I'd come to realize that religion and government — and even the medical profession — should have no say in what I freely choose to do with my own body.

By the early 1980s, I'd seen Derek Humphry speak at an American Humanists meeting, read his book *Jean's Way*, and joined the Hemlock Society. At that time I was in my early thirties.

In the 1990s, my favorite aunt died from cancer. She chose a hospice where her compassionate doctor kept her comatose until she finally passed on. For me, it was an example of just one more way of dying that I would not choose for myself.

Though none of my five loved ones suffered a lot of pain before their dying, there are other considerations in choosing the manner of one's own death.

Final Exit Network is the only American right-to-die group that will offer me information (which I could also get from any bookstore, public library, or Amazon), and stand by me with their supportive presence, in any one of the remaining states that has not yet legalized physician aid in dying. But more important than that is they will do the same for anyone suffering unbearably and without hope of improvement, whether that pain be mental or physical or both.

I shouldn't have to get on a plane to travel to more enlightened societies in Europe to have a death of my own choice. And until a Dignitas-type organization is available in the U.S., Final Exit Network is our next best thing.

### Jerry W.

As a teenager, I saw my mother slip away into the grips of Alzheimer's Disease and saw how it tore up our family. After five years of her not knowing anyone in the family, she had a stroke and was rushed to the hospital, only to receive treatment that allowed her to "live" five more years, in a vegetative state.

My mother's illness was not covered by any insurance. My father had to go into bankruptcy and his coping resource was alcohol, which led to his early death. There were no support groups related to Alzheimer's disease in the mid 1970s. There was no support or direction provided by any of her physicians. I vowed at that time to do whatever I could to understand why there was poor end of life care and no education for our family.

I became a Registered Nurse and set a course for myself to educate families about choices for acceptance or refusal of health care and choices related to the end of life. I joined Final Exit Network to learn how to encourage others to have the difficult discussions before a crisis hits, and to educate others about opportunities to have compassion at the end of life so one can have a death with dignity.

### Dean M.

Like many of you, I have witnessed, first-hand, the "dying process" of so many people I have loved. And how degrading and embarrassing it must be for those who are in the final stages of that process — to not have the strength, the will, nor the power to control anything, most importantly, life itself. As those I have loved were in that final process, I cried and cried, not only for losing them from my life, but most importantly the process that society has dictated to be appropriate and humane! How sad!

For the most part, we are a compassionate society. We are considerate and attentive to the wishes and needs of others. No individual, religious organization nor government has the right to determine our individual desires when it involves making that final decision — an End-Of-Life Choice. I applaud and support, wholeheartedly, the goals of this organization.

### Paul S.

My family has always believed in hastened death rather than prolonging a life without any acceptable quality. My brain-dead father's life was extended several times despite his medical power of attorney to the contrary.

My first wife died in pain from cancer. After cutting off nutrition, she survived for over a week. She never left her bed in over a month. It was anything but dignified.

### John F.

My awareness that there must be a better way to die began 30 years ago as my mother begged me to end her pain and suffering. She had made me promise long before there was a need. However, when the time came, I was powerless.

Work and a busy life followed. My involvement with Final Exit started when a good friend of mine who was a member asked me to be in a meeting with him and a representative from the Network to discuss his end of life wishes. I still have the letter he wrote to me on his final day.

### J'Fleur L.

Although I regularly attended the Episcopal Church in childhood, as a young adult I had found no personal proof of or relationship with a god. In college I studied world religions and became interested in things spiritual. Yet, I still ended up as an atheist.

However, the fear of death frequently overshadowed my joy in life. As I examined this fear, I realized that the fear was more about dying than about being dead. Somewhere in my 40s, I joined the Hemlock Society, hoping to have the means easily available to fall asleep into death peacefully.

I supported the Oregon euthanasia effort with a $20 monthly check for years and have continued my determination with the aid and support of Final Exit Network to choose self deliverance. As a result, I no longer fear dying.

### Gary Mi.

From the very day I was born, almost 76 years ago, restrictions have been heaped upon me and my activities in ever increasing numbers. There is nothing more precious or personal than how an individual elects to die. Happily, Final Exit Network is playing a significant role in this magnificent movement. With individuals all over the nation like John Abraham we can take comfort that a momentous change is in the wind.

### Tim L.

The right to choose how I die is not always supported by society, the medical profession, or our culture. Seeing my aunt live in a vegetative state for many years from a type of dementia, and experiencing my dad suffer his last years from the ravages of Parkinson's disease, deeply affected my view of dying. For me, the respect of our individual liberty means allowing each person to live a good death according to their own choices.

Soon after I found the Final Exit Network with its support of individual liberty, I became a member, and have been grateful to our local group for its classes on how to be a good advocate and how to end one's life peacefully. The right to die is important and especially relevant at this time in history as our population becomes older and the process of dying often becomes long and difficult. *(Author's note: It was Tim who coined my favorite description: "Deliberate Life Completion.")*

### Gary Ma.

When I was diagnosed with Parkinson's Disease in 1998, I had a very clear picture of what I was facing. My wife and I had cared for her mother, who also suffered from Parkinson's. For thirteen years we watched as a vivacious, active woman change into a skeletal recluse. Later, as a member of support groups in both Minnesota and Arizona, I saw people with Parkinson's in every stage of the disease. I visited many of them who were in the end stage, unable to do anything for themselves and requiring 24/7, one-on-one nursing care.

These experiences had a profound effect on me. I made up my mind that I would not let that happen to me. Joining FEN (Final Exit Network), reading the materials, attending lectures and developing close relationships with other FEN members has given me the information I needed to have confidence in my decision.

I am grateful that my wife honors my right to choose how I exit. She also makes it clear that she's in it for the long haul and that I can count on her to always be at my side should I change my plans.

I appreciate her love and willingness to stand by me, but that is not going to happen. When I am no longer able to care for myself, and what remains ahead of me is just living until I die, I will choose when and where I will go through the portal — and do it with dignity.

### My Own Story

The reason I got involved with the right to die movement is really quite simple. I was brought up believing in "liberty and justice for all." As far as I was concerned, "all" included human beings who were dying. When the Hemlock Society was formed, I joined. And I joined as a lifetime member because I knew full well, over forty years ago, that I would have that same commitment to "liberty and justice" today.

By 1980 I had been working in parishes for seven years, had founded two hospices, and had taught Death Education at Auburn University for three years. As a priest, I'd had the privilege to enter the intimacy of peoples' lives, and deaths. Already I had seen too many people die in ways that were against their wishes: in needless pain and suffering, with great distress to themselves and to all who loved them. Something had to change.

Speaking of change, I have studied and taught change theory. Making changes can be difficult, and my experience is that churches are very slow to change. I'm reminded of this joke about the dead light bulb: "How many Episcopalians does it take to change a light bulb?" Answer: "Three: one to put in the new bulb and two to stand there and mournfully proclaim 'Oh, but I really liked the old one!'"

Over the years, several parishioners have asked, "As a priest, how can you favor people 'playing God' by hastening death?" I continue to reply: "How can people dare to intervene in others' lives, and deaths, thereby abrogating the freedom God has given to each individual?" It is not up to us to act upon others as they die. God gave us all the freedom to think, to make informed decisions. Why should that freedom be diminished in the face of death any more than throughout life?

In short, I joined the Hemlock Society simply because it was the right thing to do. Over the years I've enjoyed the challenges of championing the dying, and I now enjoy the challenges of leading the Arizona affiliate of Final Exit Network.

# 4 Playing God

*Synonyms for Playing God: Mercy Killing, Assisted Suicide, Euthanasia, Pulling the Plug.*

— Roget's *21st Century Thesaurus*

I RECENTLY GAVE A SERMON at a Unitarian church explaining the theological justification for being "right with God" in one's decision to have deliberate life completion. In this chapter, I'll discuss some of the salient points.[1]

Most objectors to the right to die stand on religious grounds, claiming that God gave life and only God can take life away. Also, any deliberate ending of life is breaking the sixth commandment and therefore a mortal sin. Life is sacred and must be preserved at all costs, only God can decide when and how our lives will end, and Christians are supposed to suffer because it allows them to empathize with Jesus' suffering.

This interpretation of the sixth commandment is, in fact, wrong. Rather than "thou shall not kill," the original Hebrew translates to "thou shall not murder." Murder is "the deliberate taking of another's life, with malice." If I ask you to support me in ending my life, you are not "taking" my life and "malice" would certainly not be involved. You are merely honoring my request to end my suffering.

I happen to believe in a loving God. And I think that one can either believe in a loving God or a God who controls everything that happens to us, but you can't have it both ways. The New Testament is all about love. The loving God I believe in does not inflict or endorse suffering!

Now look at "atonement theory," the notion that Jesus died and suffered for your sins. I believe that allowing or, God forbid, encouraging someone to suffer is not pious. It is sadistic.

Just as people in a bad car accident need to be freed from their metal prison using the Jaws of Life, so a person may need help being freed from a body that has become a prison. You have the right to physically die because you

[1] If you would like to view this, about 23 minutes of my sermon about Final Exit Network, with about 13 minutes of questions and answers, are on YouTube, can be found at *https://www.youtube.com/watch?v=B5DYF9AN46o.*

have the right to be free. While death is inevitable, suffering at life's end need not be.

When opponents of the right to die say that hastening one's death is "playing God," I rebut such claims by maintaining that "playing God" is to abrogate the freedom God gave us to make our own carefully informed decisions: decisions about how we live our lives, including how we might end our lives. Are the use of a breathing machine or artificial lungs, artificial hydration and nutrition, artificial hearts and other organs, or artificial blood not "playing God"?

Here is an example of that argument, which I firmly reject:

> God has reserved to Himself the right to determine the end of life, because He alone knows the goal to which it is His will to lead it. It is for Him alone to justify a life or to cast it away.
>
> — Dietrich Bonhoeffer

The primary institutional opposition to our having the right to die comes from the Catholic Church, which has spent millions of dollars in efforts to block the passage of Physician Aid in Dying legislation. The opposition is joined by others on the religious right.

I rather like, and wholeheartedly agree with, the following excerpts from an interview with Episcopal Bishop John Shelby Spong, the eighth Bishop of Newark, as published in an Agor Media mailing in January, 2006:

**Q:** A prominent, mainline Christian who endorses aid in dying is rare. Have you always held that view? If not, when and why did you adopt it?

**A:** As a priest and bishop for more than forty years I have been privileged to live with people on their journeys through life and into death. I learned much in that process. I value, indeed treasure life. I see it as a gift of God. I have no desire to hasten its end prematurely. At the same time I see no value in extending life beyond the limits of meaningful relationships. To me life is honored when it can be laid down in an appropriate manner at the appropriate time. I defend the right of every individual to determine what that manner and time are for him or her. I see no conflict between this and my religious convictions.

**Q:** Many Christians find it difficult to reconcile their beliefs with the idea of hastening death. What do you tell them?

**A:** Hastening death is not the way I would describe my point of view. Seeing death as natural, not something evil, sinful, or even to be avoided is what I support. I seek to embrace death as a friend

> and not to be so committed to avoiding it that I cling to existence when it has ceased to be life. A breathing cadaver is not a witness to the goodness of life.

I also concur with these excerpts from Bishop Spong's address to the Hemlock Society national convention in 2003:

> It is one thing to expand life and it is quite another to postpone death. When medical science shifts from expanding the life and quality of life and begins simply to postpone the reality of death, why are we not capable of saying that the sacredness of life is no longer being served.... Do we human beings, including those of us who claim to be Christian, not have the right to say "that is not the way I choose to die?"

I believe we do. I prefer to think of death not as an enemy, but as a friend, even a brother, as St. Francis of Assisi once suggested. The time has come, I believe, for Christians to embrace death not as an enemy to be defeated but as an aspect of life's holiness to be embraced. Death is life's shadow. It walks with us through the entire course of our days.

We embrace death as a friend because we honor life. I honor the God of Life by living fully. I do not honor this God by clinging to a life that has become an empty shell. ... The God whom I experience as a Source of Life can surely not be served by those in whom death is simply postponed after real life has departed. I also think the choice to do so should be acclaimed as both moral and ethical, a human right if you will.

# Tools to Help You Explore Your Attitudes and Experiences

# 5

*Life is pleasant. Death is peaceful.*
*It's the transition that's troublesome.*

— Isaac Asimov

This short section is for self-assessment. Most people have not given a lot of detailed thought to the subject of death. Where do you stand? Where to start? This is not a test, but an exercise to help you to organize your own questions, thoughts, attitudes, feelings, and beliefs about death.

## Thoughts

Read the following statements, and ask yourself how each relates to your personal beliefs.

- I believe in some form of life after death.
- I believe that you die when your number comes up. It's in the hands of fate.
- I believe that taking one's own life is never justified, justified when terminally ill, or justified whenever life no longer seems worth living.
- I believe that taking another person's life is never justified, justified in the defense of your own life, or justified when the person has committed a terrible crime.
- I believe that dying people should be told the truth about their condition, kept hopeful by sparing them the facts, or it depends on the person and the circumstances.
- In thinking about my own old age, I would prefer to die before I grow old, to live as long as I can, or to discover what challenges and opportunities old age will bring for me.
- A person has been taken to the emergency room with internal bleeding that is likely to prove fatal. This person is eighty-two years of age, and has an Alzheimer-type dementia. What type of response would you recommend from the emergency room staff if this were

you or a loved one? Comfort only, a limited attempt at rescue, or an all-out rescue attempt?

- Another round of chemotherapy has failed to halt advanced breast cancer. The doctor suggests a new round of chemotherapy. The patient replies, "I wish I were dead." What do you think should be done — and why?

## Feelings

Again, this is a self-assessment.

- Would you feel comfortable in an intimate conversation with a dying person?
- Would you hesitate to touch someone who is dying?
- Would you have more difficulty in talking if the dying person was about your age?
- Would you avoid talking about death and dying with a person who is terminally ill?
- Would you avoid talking with a dying person if possible?
- Have you had moments of anxiety in which you think of your own death?
- Do you fear that you will die soon?
- Do you have no fear of death?
- Do you feel good when you think about life after death?
- Are you anxious about the possible death of someone you love?
- Are you grieving over somebody who has already died?
- Do you have a hard time taking death seriously; it feels remote to you, not really connected with your own life?
- Do you have some strong, even urgent feelings regarding death these days?

## Death Experiences

The following questions may help you determine how ready you are to accept the death of someone you love, or your own impending death:

- Have you ever had an animal companion that died? If so, how did that make you feel?
- Have other people who were important to you died? If so, how long ago?

- If you have known more than one person who has died, which one affected you most? What kinds of feelings were you left with? Afterward, what were your most positive memories?
- What are your most disturbing memories?
- Have you conversed with dying people? If so, how many?
- Have you provided care for a dying person?
- Have you known a person who has attempted suicide but survived?
- Have you known a person who succeeded in committing suicide?
- Have you known someone who hastened their death with the aid of a physician?
- Have you known someone who died in an accident?
- Have you known someone who was murdered?
- Who/When/Under what circumstances did your most recent death experience occur?
- How many more years do you anticipate you will live?
- What life-threatening or life-endangering behaviors do you engage in? (E.g., fast driving, no seat belts, unwise diet, excessive drinking, smoking, etc.)
- If you could choose it, where and how would you prefer your death to occur?
- What is your preferred mode of body disposition at death?
- What, if any, expectations do you have for "afterlife"?
- Have you made a will yet? If yes, what is the relationship of the primary beneficiary?
- At what age do you consider that death for a person is no longer "premature"?

I hope you find the above helpful in assessing your own background and beliefs. I'll never try to tell you what to think. Even if you firmly believe that you will want to be kept alive with life-support equipment, I urge others to honor your beliefs, because it is your life. And I would hope that you would also honor mine.

# 6 The Death Taboo

In any discussion of the topic, it helps to begin by calling it what it is: death. All too often we avoid using the "D" words: death, dying, dead (oh my, is it a four-letter-word?), die or died (yikes, another four-letter-word!). Jennifer Worth described this phenomenon in her book *In the Midst of Life*:

> It is well nigh impossible to talk to anyone about death, I find. Most people seem deeply embarrassed. It is like when I was a girl and nobody could talk about sex. We all did it, but nobody talked about it! We have now grown out of that silly taboo, and we must grow out of our inhibitions surrounding death. They have arisen largely because so few people see death any more, even though it is quite obviously in our midst. A cultural change must come, a new atmosphere of freedom, which will only happen if we open our closed minds.

Once I attended a reception following a funeral at which a couple of hundred people were gathered. Although all were there to express their condolences to the family of the deceased, as I lingered near the receiving line I did not hear one sympathizer use a "D" word. Several said, "I'm sorry for your loss," which can also be comforting, since by far the number one concern of those bereaved is simply to have their loss be recognized. But not one person said "I'm sorry that Joseph died."

This is typical. We call death anything but what it really is, and in doing so I believe we do ourselves a disservice. Numerous quotidian euphemisms abound: My list of euphemisms extends to several hundred as found in Appendix L. The English language contains numerous euphemisms related to dying, death, burial, and the people and places that deal with death. The practice of using euphemisms for death is likely to have originated with the superstition that to speak the word "death" was to invite death, where to "draw death's attention" is the ultimate bad fortune. A common theory holds that death is a taboo subject in most English-speaking cultures for precisely this reason. It may be said that one is not dying, but fading quickly because the end is near. People who have died are described as having passed away or passed or departed.

One euphemism I hear frequently is "expired." It seems that nurses in particular are prone to using this one, to which I say that parking meters and drivers licenses expire; people die. In Sedona, known as the New Age capital of our country, apparently people don't die — they have a "celestial discharge." Another of my favorites is the bureaucratic phrase explaining that the patient experienced a "negative patient-care outcome." To use terms other than "D" words only serves to perpetuate our fear and misunderstanding of death and to further our death-denying society and our death-phobic culture.

Leo Tolstoy famously mocked the denial of death in *The Death of Ivan Ilyich:*

> In the depths of his soul Ivan Ilyich knew that he was dying...he simply did not, he could not possibly understand it. The example of a syllogism he had studied in Kiesewetter's logic — Caius is a man, men are mortal, therefore Caius is mortal — had seemed to him all his life to be correct only in relation to Caius, but by no means himself. For the man Caius, man in general, it was perfectly correct; but he was not Caius and not man in general, he had always been quite, quite separate from all other human beings.... And Caius is indeed mortal, and it's right that he die, but for me, Vanya, Ivan Ilyich, with all my feelings and thoughts — for me it's another matter. And it cannot be that I should die. It would be too terrible.
>
> So it felt to him.

Here are a couple of additional recent quotations on our avoidance of death:

> Death is not good. It's just a fact. We don't need to give it so much importance. So I don't want to read anything that talks about it.
>
> — Aditi Bose

> I've adopted the guideline of Warren Buffett's partner, Charlie Munger, who says, "I wanna know where I'll be when I die — so I never go there."
>
> — Tom Brokaw

## Death Education for Children

As I reflect on ways that learning about death and dying may benefit us, I wonder why I did not learn more about death as a young child. Might there be some way to introduce constructive conversations about death to children?

Most parents are more comfortable dealing with children's happy emotions than their sad ones. We like our children's stories to have happy endings, even though there aren't always happy endings in life, and emotions are not always upbeat.

A professor of the positive psychology movement has suggested that many meaningful feelings are evoked by depressing, stressful or even horrific stories. Contrary to what many people believe, watching sad or tragic tales can actually put us more in touch with our humanity and improve our feelings of gratitude and well-being.

Answering a child's questions about death with empathy and gentleness, at the child's level of understanding, demystifies the subject and can help calm fears. Maybe the child wants to know why and how a pet died, or why a wild bird is now motionless. What children want most is to understand, and forthright answers can help a great deal.

I would go so far as to say that discussing death with children could somehow even be playful. With that in mind about sixteen years ago, I developed an idea for some toys to teach death education. My name for these is the "Thanatological Mighty Morbidities." Sure, it's a mouthful, but so is "Teenage Mutant Ninja Turtles."

The Morbidities would be three-dimensional action figures packaged in a brown cardboard box in the hexagonal traditional shape of a wooden coffin. Each would contain a card with the story line and the educational information. A marketing slogan might be "Get real! Get dead!"

The back stories of each would have educational value. For example, Minister Mike, with hair standing on end after being struck by lightning, would offer education on the dangers of lightning and how to protect yourself from it. Nurse Nancy, flattened by tire tracks after being run over by an ambulance, would offer traffic safety information. Others might include Policeman Paul, riddled with gunshots, Logger Larry, crushed by a fallen tree, Shark-Swallowed Sam, Drunk Driver Donna, Miner Mitch, SIDS Suzy, Choking Charlie, Lawyer Larry having been knifed in the back, Drowned Deborah, Burning Betsy, Poisoned Peter, and so on.

Do the Thanatological Mighty Morbidities have a "gore factor?" Yes! That is part of our fascination with death: We all slow down and stare when passing a bad car wreck. Surely, at least, every red-blooded boy ages 6 to 14 will want the Thanatological Mighty Morbidities! So may many adults! The media and parents will grimace at, maybe prohibit, and generally frown upon such toys, thus perhaps making them all the more appealing to kids!

My hope would be that such toys would prompt both children and adults to begin to discuss the reality of death as part of life in realistic terms, thus lessening our continuation of the death taboo.

## Why Learn About Death?

> There ought to be at least as much common sense about living and dying as there is about going to the grocery store and buying a loaf of bread.
>
> — Dalton Trumbo, *Johnny Got His Gun*

This has been my car license plate for about a decade. With only seven characters permitted in Arizona, it proclaims "WE ALL DIE."

> We are all dying one by one. We all smell of mortality, and we can't wash it off.
>
> — Siri Hustvedt, *The Summer Without Men*

> We defy augury. There is special providence in the fall of a sparrow. If it be now, 'tis not to come; if it be not to come, it will be now; if it be not now, yet it will come — the readiness is all. Since no man, of aught he leaves, knows what is't to leave betimes, let be.
>
> — William Shakespeare, *Hamlet*

As a natural, inevitable part of life's course, we see death depicted in music, literature, film, television, and fine arts. And death is taken into account in such fields as theology, economics, law, psychology, sociology, philosophy, cultural anthropology, medicine, and others. Young people, especially, sorely need an objective and comprehensive kind of education informing their understanding of death.

I often hear the term "closure" when referring to those grieving, or in mourning. I avoid that term. The issue is not closed because we have not forgotten the ones we loved.

The church sometimes tries, but it is not the best vehicle for death education. Christian denominations and other religions vary widely in their beliefs, and some take strong positions on such issues as abortion, euthanasia, and afterlife, which would distort objective death education.

Death education is not part of the typical family agenda. When it comes to the one crisis all people will confront, parents become mute. Embarrassed prudery and frightened withdrawal are manifest from our own gnawing anxieties about death. Because death makes people uncomfortable, we evade the issue or, by partially informing, succeed only in misinforming. Too often we meet inquiries about death with evasion and denial.

One of my goals is to seek to clarify the understanding of death. I posit that as we learn about death, we might gently remove the taboo aspect of death language, enabling all of us to read and discourse upon death rationally, thereby lessening anxiety.

## Other Reasons for a Formal Education about Death

Among other benefits, death education can help us to:

- Assist the individual in developing a personal eschatology by specifying the relationship between life and death.
- Understand the dynamics of grief and mourning and the reactions of differing age groups to the death of a "significant other."
- Promote comfortable and intelligent interaction with the dying as human beings that are, indeed, living until they are dead.
- Educate students about death so they grow with a minimum of death-related anxieties, which are too often based upon irrationality and myth rather than fact.
- Understand the role of those involved in the death system and the assets and liabilities of that system.
- Educate consumers to the commercial death market.
- Recognize the variations involved in aspects of death both within and among cultures.
- Cultivate a more realistic comprehension of the consequences of behaviors such as drunk driving, consuming drugs, smoking and other risky and life-threatening acts.
- Know the false idols and mythology existing in the growing field of death study, the salient heuristic questions, and the great need for learning more.

Furthermore, I postulate that the death-educated person:

- Communicates more effectively, honestly, and openly on intimate matters with loved ones and others.

- Acts to attain his/her life's priorities and values, and consequently improve health in a self-actualizing sense.
- Recognizes, values and supports those aspects of society that will promote the health of children, the aged and other vulnerable groups.
- Relinquishes control more easily, resulting in a more satisfying, appropriate death for one's self, and a healthier bereavement for death-educated survivors.
- Is likely to espouse alternatives to conflict-resolution other than violence, war, and related forms of species-specific deadly aggression. In *Extremely Loud and Incredibly Close*, Jonathan Safron Foer wrote: "She died in my arms saying, 'I don't want to die.' That is what death is like. It doesn't matter what uniforms the soldiers are wearing. It doesn't matter how good the weapons are. I thought if everyone could see what I saw, we could never have war anymore."
- Acts to effect positive and healthy social and environmental changes.

# Honoring Death by Recognizing its Benefits

# 7

*I do not honor life when I fail to see that death and finitude are what gives life its precious quality. Death is not a punishment for sin, as Paul also once suggested and as classical Christianity has long maintained. Death is an aspect of life, a vital aspect that gives life its deepest flavor, its defining sensitivity.*

— Episcopal Bishop John Spong

THIS CHAPTER IS A BIT of a twist on how we might regard the reality of death. In case all of this thus far has been too negative, pessimistic, or morbid for you, I thought I might add some reflections about the actual benefits of death. Not financial "death benefits" but what we may view as positive aspects of human death.

For most of us who are committed to end-of-life choices, death is something to which we have reconciled ourselves, and for which we have prepared. For some people it is a rude surprise, a tragic event, or the Grim Reaper. For others it may be release and relief. For physicians, it is usually a defeat. I am sure that you can readily add more examples of different attitudes toward death.

Death may not yet be your friend, but whether you accept it or rage against it, I think it is worthwhile to ponder some of the positive aspects of striving to meet death with peace. My aim in this book, and in my work, is to make the reality of death more satisfactory, more humane, more tolerable, and more comforting for every individual who will die.

Raging against death is, of course, one's prerogative. I am reminded of the poem *Do Not Go Gentle into That Good Night* by Dylan Thomas. He speaks of old age, wise men, good men, wild men, grave men, all raging against the dying of the light. It is a poignant reminder of the finitude of the time we have.

Is it possible that death may be beneficial? Of course, death can be unsettling, troubling, unpleasant, inconvenient, ugly, frightening and otherwise disturbing. But it can also be regarded as natural and helpful.

Saint Ambrose addresses this in his book *On the Benefits of Death.* He begins, "Why is death not an evil, since it is so contrary to life?" On this he distinguishes three sorts of death: the death which occasions sin and murders the soul; the death of sin, which he calls a mystic death; and the natural death, which terminates the course of life and separates the soul from the body. We acknowledge that the first sort of death is a great evil, as the second is a great good. It is not so with the third. We see that death is gain, life is loss. Paul says:

> *For me life is Christ, and death a gain.* What does "Christ" mean but to die in the body, and receive the breath of life? Let us then die with Christ, to live with Christ. We should have a daily familiarity with death, a daily desire for death. By this kind of detachment our soul must learn to free itself from the desires of the body. It must soar above earthly lusts to a place where they cannot come near, to hold it fast. It must take on the likeness of death, to avoid the punishment of death. The law of our fallen nature is at war with the law of our reason and subjects the law of reason to the law of error. What is the remedy? *Who will set me free from this body of death? The grace of God, through Jesus Christ, our Lord.*

In October of 2009 I attended a talk by His Holiness The Dalai Lama in Washington D.C., where I had first met him in 1976. After his talk an audience member asked, "Do you think death is good or bad?" He responded this way:

> First of all, we should realize that death is truly part of life and that it is neither good nor bad in itself. In *The Tibetan Book of the Dead,* it says "What we called death is merely a concept." In other words, death represents the end of the gross consciousness and its support, the gross body.
>
> This happens at the gross level of the mind. But neither death nor birth exist at the subtle level of consciousness that we call "clear light." …It is important that during our lifetime we become familiar with the idea of death, so that it will not be a real shock to us at the moment it comes….
>
> I think the most important thing is to try and do our best to ensure that dying persons may depart quietly, with serenity and in a peace. The just regard it as fortunate, and others fear it as a dreadful punishment. This fear arises only from our weakness, and from the illusions which the false pleasures of life present us with. To dissipate this fear, we must consider how many afflictions, bitternesses, chagrins, cares, temptations, perils, etc., we are surrounded with in this world, and that the longer we remain in it we shall augment the number of our sins.

He then shows that with death delivering us from all these evils, it should be regarded as an advantage, and that we should not therefore fear it.

## Death as a Gift to Life

> Death twitches my ear; "Live," he says… "I'm coming."
>
> — Virgil

This section describes several ways in which death may be considered a gift to life.

### 1. Death gives deeper meaning and inspiration to life.

In the *Iliad*, Achilles says:

> I'll tell you a secret. Something they don't teach you in your temple. The Gods envy us. They envy us because we're mortal, because any moment might be our last. Everything is more beautiful because we're doomed. You will never be lovelier than you are now. We will never be here again.

Knowing death's reality may mean a heightened awareness of life's limitations and uncertainties. This knowledge may help one to cope in the real world. And such knowledge may serve to better one's recognition, value and support of those aspects of society that promote the care of children, the aged, the infirm, and other vulnerable groups.

Kurt Vonnegut says, "We are here for no purpose, unless we can invent one. I tell you, we are here on Earth to fart around, and don't let anybody tell you any different." But I believe this from Morrie Schwartz: "All right. Now here's the payoff. Here is how we are different from those wonderful plants and animals. As long as we can love each other, and remember the feeling of love we had, we can die without ever really going away. All the love you created is still there. All the memories are still there. You live on — in the hearts of everyone you have touched and nurtured while you were here."

The tireless French actress Sarah Bernhardt went through more than a thousand lovers in her colorful life, many of them famous writers and artists. She once observed, "It is by spending oneself that one becomes rich." Bernhardt often slept in a rosewood coffin lined with letters from her lovers.

Of course, people have diverse ideas on death's meaning. Here are a few quotations worth pondering:

From Leo Rosten:

> Where was it ever promised us that life on this earth can ever be easy, free from conflict and uncertainty, devoid of anguish and wonder and pain? Those who seek the folly of unrelieved "happiness" — who fear moods, who shun solitude, who do not know the dignity of occasional depression — can find bliss easily enough: in tranquilizing pills, or in senility. The purpose of life is not to be happy.

From John Cage:

> No why. Just here. Death, the unavoidable ending of life, is a catalyst for change in life. It gives us a constant kick up the backside and gets us working towards our goals in life.

From Richard Feynman:

> I don't have to know an answer. I don't feel frightened by not knowing things, by being lost in the mysterious universe without having any purpose, which is the way it really is, as far as I can tell, possibly. It doesn't frighten me.

From Alexa Stevenson:

> The ending shouldn't determine the meaning of anything, a story or a life. Logically, I don't think it can — didn't Heidegger say something to that effect? That the meaning of all our moments cannot be contingent upon an end-point over which we have no control? That if we are happy right now, that means something, even if we die tomorrow? Narrative integrity is overrated. I don't need to know that the story of my life has a happy ending to enjoy it. A good thing, too, because I hear all the characters die in the end.

### 2. Death literally gives us life.

What do we eat? Formerly living plants and animals. Death contributes to the cosmic plasma, nourishing and enriching the lifeblood of creation. $E=mc^2$. Matter is not lost but rather transformed.

A presenter at the 1997 Nobel Conference noted that "all the molecules in your body were formed inside stars. We are the future of ancient stars."

In fact there is a growing movement in the United States toward natural burial, wherein a body is simply placed into the earth, as it's the most efficient way for humans to return their body's nutrients to the ecosystem. Walt Whitman said: "I bequeath myself to the dirt to grow from the grass I love. If you want me again look for me under your boot-soles."

There are more pragmatic ways that death contributes to life: The University of Tennessee's Forensic Anthropology Center (The Body Farm) helps us to determine the cause of death and the time of death, information that can be helpful in solving crime, and methods to locate buried or clandestine bodies.

Another gift is that almost all major organs can be donated and transplanted: pancreas, liver, lungs, heart, intestines, and kidneys. And tissues can also be reused to enhance and extend other people's lives: veins, heart valves, corneas, ligaments, tendons, bone, nerves, and skin. I think it would be good if we established body farms for the purpose of harvesting these from newly dead bodies.

### 3. Death enables evolution.

> What is it that dies? A log of wood dies to become a few planks. The planks die to become a chair. The chair dies to become a piece of firewood, and the firewood dies to become ash. You give different names to the different shapes the wood takes, but the basic substance is there always. If we could always remember this, we would never worry about the loss of anything. We never lose anything; we never gain anything. By such discrimination we put an end to unhappiness.
>
> —Swami Satchidananda, "The Yoga Sutras"

The process of death leads to evolution of life forms that are better suited to the environment, it allows for interdependent diversity, and it contributes to progress through social and cultural evolution. Our world is ongoing, and if our species is to survive for another five billion years, evolutionary change will be required. Without the death of Neanderthals, modern humans would not exist.

Without the reality of death we would still resemble amoebas or protozoans in a mud puddle. Without death, variety in life would not exist. We need the chain of life: the rabbit to eat the leaf, the wolf to eat the rabbit, the bear to eat the wolf, humankind to eat the bear. If the only creatures were still beetles, Swan Lake and the Sistine Chapel would not exist.

Also among these evolutionary gifts, new ideas and institutions evolve and emerge as the old die. To believe that this planet is round means to discard the notion of a flat earth. The end of horse-drawn transportation means the convenience of automobile travel. Societal and cultural evolution are also enhanced by death. Human death may have further socially redeeming value: our population is kept in balance, and economic and social opportunities are renewed through attrition.

Taking evolution even further, who knows, perhaps in the centuries ahead we may develop the capacity to regularly communicate with those who have died. And there are many physicists who believe in the existence of other dimensions beyond our customary understanding of a four dimensional universe. This is yet to be proven, of course, but maybe the dead reside in a parallel universe!

### 4. Sensitivity to death means an appreciation of how fragile life is.

Knowing death's reality may mean a heightened awareness of life's limitations and uncertainties. This knowledge may help one to cope in the real world. And such knowledge may serve to better one's recognition, value and support of those aspects of society that promote the care of children, the aged, the infirm, and other vulnerable groups.

**5. In a similar vein, death is the reminder of our common human condition.**

Nobody escapes death. It is the great equalizer, coming to king and peasant, rich and poor, just and unjust, black and white, homosexual and heterosexual, educated and ignorant. Death recognizes no differences, exercises no prejudice.

**6. Healthy adjustment to death may facilitate good adaptations to other losses.**

Life is filled with lesser phenomenological losses such as the breakup of a relationship, moving to a new town, no longer having good vision, loss of a job, and many more. Grappling with the ultimate loss may lessen the burden of smaller losses, and vice versa.

**7. The hurt surrounding loss through death tells us we care, and we can endure loss.**

Tears are a tender tribute, evidencing love. That we care means we suffer, and such suffering testifies to our capacity to love, and to love again and again. The economy of sympathy and love is one of plenty, not scarcity. One can always be amative. We may love ten people or love ten thousand people. We may use what we have learned for the benefit of others, adapting the creative capacity and energy of love to fit ongoing life and relationships. As Winnie the Pooh says, when someone we love dies: "How lucky I am to have something that makes saying goodbye so hard."

The writer and commentator Kate O'Neill put it this way:

> Love doesn't die with death. Love is like liquid; when it pours out, it seeps into others' lives. Love changes form and shape. Love gets into everything. Death doesn't conquer all; love does. Love wins every single time. Love wins by lasting through death. Love wins by loving more, loving again, loving without fear.

Virginia Woolf, in her suicide note, wrote:

> Dearest, I feel certain that I am going mad again. I feel we can't go through another of those terrible times. And I shan't recover this time. I begin to hear voices, and I can't concentrate. So I am doing what seems the best thing to do. You have given me the greatest possible happiness. You have been in every way all that anyone could be. I don't think two people could have been happier 'til this terrible disease came. I can't fight any longer. I know that I am spoiling your life, that without me you could work. And you will I know. You see I can't even write this properly. I can't read. What I want to say is I owe all the happiness of my life to you. You have been

> entirely patient with me and incredibly good. I want to say that — everybody knows it. If anybody could have saved me it would have been you. Everything has gone from me but the certainty of your goodness. I can't go on spoiling your life any longer. I don't think two people could have been happier than we have been. V.

Moreover, many people find grieving to be a positive experience. For example, it often gives a greater appreciation for someone or something, or fills the bereaved with fond memories. The way one deals with grief is certainly influenced by one's previous life experiences: We might remember the words of Alfred Lord Tennyson who said, "I am part of all that I have met."

The pain experienced in surviving loss through death may serve as a motivator. Just as the pain of a cut tells me the wound needs attention, so emotional pain may prompt new direction in engaging with life. I know a woman who, after months of grieving in self-imposed confinement, left her home and rectified an important situation because she was angry enough to take action. Frequently, we only make major constructive changes in life when we are sufficiently uncomfortable.

### 8. The possibility of death may serve to benefit life.

Appreciating the reality and impact of death may lessen the likelihood of deadly aggression, and increase our efforts to seek alternative methods of conflict resolution. The knowledge that war brings death helps us to avoid war. We also may be less likely to engage in life-threatening behavior such as alcohol or drug abuse or smoking.

### 9. Death brings an end to suffering.

This benefit is obvious, and, as I mentioned earlier, it can also be a tremendous relief to the one suffering and to caregivers.

> I never really wanted to die. But I followed through anyway. The pain in my heart was excruciating, and death was beautiful.
>
> — Rae Hachton, *Pretty In Black*

> In her room death would come as a friend, a friend with cool gentle hands.
>
> — Mary Higgins Clark, *A Stranger Is Watching*

> Can you not see death as the friend and deliverer? It means stripping off that body which is tormenting you. What are you afraid of? Has this world been so kind to you that you should leave it with regret?
>
> — C.S. Lewis, *The Collected Letters of C. S. Lewis, Volume lll*

In *The Quiet American*, Graham Greene wrote:

> Death was the only absolute value in my world. Lose life and one would lose nothing again forever. I envied those who could believe in a God and I distrusted them. I felt they were keeping their courage up with a fable of the changeless and the permanent. Death was far more certain than God, and with death there would be no longer the daily possibility of love dying. The nightmare of a future of boredom and indifference would lift. I could never have been a pacifist. To kill a man was surely to grant him an immeasurable benefit. Oh yes, people always, everywhere, loved their enemies. It was their friends they preserved for pain and vacuity.

## 10. A final gift of death is our memories of the collective dead.

The ability to recall those who have gone before us can be advantageous. As we are enriched by the heritage of previous generations, so may we be rooted in our sense of belonging in this life. We are part of those who have gone before us. And we may be inspired to constructive change: For example, the remembrance of the evils experienced by slaves in the United States enabled us to envision and enact a better way of life, free of slavery.

And, oh my God! Where would the funeral directors, forensic pathologists, morticians, grief counselors, coroners, homicide investigators, obituary writers, thanatologists, hospices, the right-to-die movement, the coffin industry, cemeteries, crematoriums, and maybe even the flower industry, be without death?

This is a litany I have used:

Without the death of stars, there would be no planets and no life.

Without the death of creatures, there would be no evolution.

Without the death of elders, there would be no room for children.

Without the death of fetal cells, we would all be spheres.

Without the death of neurons, wisdom and creativity would not blossom.

Without the death of cells in woody plants, there would be no trees.

Without the death of forests by Ice Age advance,
there would be no northern lakes.

Without the death of mountains, there would be no sand or soil.

Without the death of plants and animals, there would be no food.

Without the death of old ways of thinking,
there would be no room for the new.

Without death, there would be no ancestors.

Without death, time would not be precious.

The gifts of death are Mars and Mercury, Saturn and Earth.
The gifts of death are the atoms of stardust within our bodies.
The gifts of death are the splendors of shape and form and color.
The gifts of death are diversity, the immense journey of life.
The gifts of death are food: the sustenance of life.
The gifts of death are seeing, hearing, feeling — deeply feeling.
The gifts of death are wisdom, creativity, and the flow of cultural change.
The gifts of death are the urgency to act, the desire to fully be and become.
The gifts of death are joy and sorrow, laughter and tears.
The gifts of death are lives that are fully and exuberantly lived, and then graciously and gratefully given up, for now and forevermore.

## A Few More Thoughts of Others

To be what we are and to become what we are able of becoming is the only end of life.

— Robert Louis Stevenson

Death is most terrifying to those who have yet to live.

— Dan Pearce, *Single Dad Laughing*

We must conquer life by living it to the full, and then we can go to meet death with a certain prestige.

— Aleister Crowley, *Diary of a Drug Fiend*

The old man smiled. "I shall not die of a cold, my son. I shall die of having lived."

— Willa Cather, *Death Comes for the Archbishop*

Happiness is not the end of life; character is.

— Henry Ward Beecher

Dying has a funny way of making you see people, the living and the dead, a little differently. Maybe that's just part of the grieving, or maybe the dead stand there and open our eyes a bit wider.

— Susan Gregg Gilmore, *Looking for Salvation at the Dairy Queen*

Death is not a tragedy to the one who dies; to have wasted the life before that death, that is the tragedy.

— Orson Scott Card, *Shadow of the Hegemon*

It is not the end of the physical body that should worry us. Rather, our concern must be to live while we're alive — to release our inner selves from the spiritual death that comes with living behind a facade designed to conform to external definitions of who and what we are.

— Elisabeth Kübler-Ross

It is appointed for man to die once, live life to the fullness.

— Lailah Gifty Akita, *The Alphabets of Success: Passion Driven Life*

# Who Owns and Directs our Dying? 8

A doctor who blogs under the pseudonym Scott Alexander at the Web site *Slate Star Codex* describes how many of his patients leave the world: "Old, limbless, bedridden, ulcerated, in a puddle of waste, gasping for breath, loopy on morphine, hopelessly demented in a sterile hospital room." He gives some sad and graphic details. Be forewarned, this gets gruesome:

> You will become bedridden, unable to walk or even to turn yourself over. You will become completely dependent on nurse assistants to intermittently shift your position to avoid pressure ulcers. When they inevitably slip up, your skin develops huge incurable sores that can sometimes erode all the way to the bone, and which are perpetually infected with foul-smelling bacteria. Your limbs will become practically vestigial organs, like the appendix, and when your vascular disease gets too bad, one or more will be amputated, sacrifices to save the host. Urinary and fecal continence disappear somewhere in the process, so you're either connected to catheters or else spend a while every day lying in a puddle of your own wastes until the nurses can help you out.

Most doctors, meanwhile, choose to die quickly and with very limited intervention from the health-care system. In *How Doctors Die*, Dr. Ken Murray writes: "I cannot count the number of times fellow physicians have told me, in words that vary only slightly, 'Promise me if you find me like this that you'll kill me.' They mean it."

For every patient who might request physician-assisted suicide, there are thousands more whose lives are being prolonged unnecessarily by hospital bureaucracies. They need our compassion and attention as well. Yet for patients near the end of life the ethical choices are often reversed.

Thousands of patients, both orally and in writing, request "do not resuscitate" designations. Basically this means, "If I am in pain, have no quality of life and I'm incapable of communicating intelligently with you, do not keep me alive by hooking me up to a respirator, feeding me through a tube or breaking my ribs with CPR so that I will continue in that condition." Yet hospitals systematically deny such requests if even one family member objects. The relative may be someone the patient hasn't seen in years. She may be someone the patient doesn't even like. This needs to end. And our attitude toward death needs to change.

Canada is wrestling with right-to-die at the time of this writing. The issue that has been an open wound of emotionalism and lack of progress is that of what is variously called euthanasia, assisted suicide, or even compassionate homicide. For a nation as progressive and authentically liberal as Canada, their lack of movement has been disastrous, and much of this can be attributed to a previous government beholden to a Christian right obsessed with the issue. It's one of the big three for them of course: No to abortion, no to gay rights, no to euthanasia. Because they have lost the first two, they are fighting like zealots to defend the last.

So what are we actually speaking about here? It's vitally important to cut through the nonsense and realize that the alternative to assisted dying is not living; the alternative to assisted dying is unassisted dying. Dying in pain, anguish and frequently in isolation. Death is always inevitable and while we must do all in our power to preserve life, the quality of that life is a major factor.

Quality of life, however, is a politically loaded term. Disability does not denote lack of quality, daily struggle does not denote lack of quality, age does not denote lack of quality. We once revered the elderly as mansions of wisdom, but now they are sometimes seen as slums that are better off demolished. So a civilized society must be extremely careful in how it regards the elderly, the unfit and the unhealthy.

But this is not really the issue at hand, and anybody who tells you otherwise is misleading you. Imagine knowing without any doubt that you have a few months, perhaps a year, to live and that most of that time will be experienced — despite loads of medication — in daily agony. Or consider someone with a neurological disease, their muscles and movement are wasting away yet their mind is still functioning and they know that one day they will drown within their own body and that there is nothing that can be done. This is the tear-stained, horrific reality of the argument.

None of this is easy, all of this is profound, but a majority of people now agree that a regulated, supervised system of assisted dying is the only humane approach. Teams of doctors and family members would have to concur with the individual's wishes, time would be required for repeated consideration, every single circumstance would be analyzed. But in the name of God — and I use the word deliberately — we can no longer stand by and allow such suffering to continue due to a theological or philosophical technicality.

Ignore the political hysteria about depressed teenagers being killed in Europe or terrible mistakes taking place in Oregon where people are euthanized against their wishes. These are false excuses, based on supposed events that are not happening. The Dutch example is probably the best example. Of those who request to die in the Netherlands, one-third are declined, another third die before their case is decided, and the remaining third are indeed helped to an early death.

I heard this tale from a fellow who will never forget his father's final few days in hospital. The father, who had experienced the Second World War in Bomber Command and who knew the flesh, blood and rawness of life, was fully aware that after his second stroke and his continuing cancer he had very little time left. He wanted to go. He turned his head to his son and mouthed a few words that will always remain private between them. But there was nothing the son could do. The father survived for a little longer, in a drug-induced haze of pain or indifference. That wasn't a death he deserved. It's not a death anybody deserves.

A friend recently told me about the horrible experience of her father's death, with all kinds of unwanted and unnecessary medical interventions postponing the inevitable. I was luckily spared a similar experience when my father died peacefully at age ninety-six in 2008. He refused to go to the hospital because he knew better. He had been the executive director of the hospital! He died peacefully in a care home, with me holding his hand and telling him it was alright to die, and he said he was ready to die.

Leading up to that point, after caring for my father at home as long as possible, I first put him in what was reputed to be the best nursing home in town: fancy and expensive. Within two weeks it became clear that he was not getting the attention he needed and deserved. After placing him in yet another inadequate facility, I finally found a great place about twenty miles down the road, which was run by Mennonites. There, the staff actually gave a damn about him and he was quite comfortable and well cared for, as should have been the case in the first two institutions.

My mother had died in a nursing home in 1999 at age eighty-three. For eight years she had Alzheimer's disease, which, at the time, no one knew was fatal. My parents were deeply devoted to each other and my father cared for her at home as long as he was able. Her dying was an extremely frightening experience for her. She was a brilliant woman, a Smith College alumnus with a graduate degree, and had served as the head of the modern language department of a local college. Yet in the end she was trapped in her failing body with a failing mind. She did not even know who I was as she approached death.

Having visited countless assisted living facilities and nursing homes myself, I am pretty sure I shall never be a resident therein. Most of them seem like mere warehouses for elderly people who do not want to be there, feeling isolated and trapped. Dr. Atul Gawande says:

> People experience these as prisons. As people get older they get lower levels of anxiety, higher levels of happiness, until you put them into these institutions, and then that's when you see the three plagues of loneliness, helplessness, and boredom. You know, people don't want to play bingo and be comfortable all the time. They want to know that they have some things that connect them to who they are. But that is not what families are asking about. And so the result is that we get places that end up reconstructed to look more and more like hospitals, instead of like homes where you can go to the kitchen and get what you like.

I read recently that eldercare facilities are not marketed to the potential residents but rather to their children, mostly baby-boomers, who will be making the decision to put a parent or grandparent there. Therefore, many of the facilities are elegant and spic-and-span, but that does not tell you much about the quality of care.

There are some notable exceptions to Dr. Gawande's description. For example, The Villas at Green Valley, in Arizona, provides 6,000-square-foot houses that are furnished and beautifully decorated. Each house has ten private suites with individual bathrooms and HVAC systems. In other words, each resident has only nine housemates in what looks like a large ten-bedroom house. They also boast a 1:5 caregiver ratio with multiple levels of care available. And, indeed, one may snack from the kitchen or the pantry.

## Changes in Medical Culture Needed

Unwanted treatment is a particularly confounding problem because it is not a product of malevolence but a by-product of two strengths of American medical culture: the system's determination to save lives, and its technological virtuosity. Change will need to be consonant with that culture. You have to be comfortable working at the margins of the power structure within medicine, and particularly within academic medicine. You need a disrupter who can speak the language of medicine and meet the system on its own terms.

It is easy to find fault with both doctors and patients with regard to our culture of tortured dying, but in many ways all the parties are simply victims of a larger system that encourages excessive treatment. Is it any wonder that doctors feel compelled to practice "cover your ass" medicine these days? In some unfortunate cases, doctors use the fee-for-service model to do everything they can, no matter how pointless, to make more money. More commonly, though, doctors are fearful of litigation and do whatever they are asked, with little feedback, to avoid getting in trouble. Even when the right preparations have been made, the system can still swallow people up.

Said one doctor: "Too often, we doctors are practicing irrational medicine at the end of life. We are like cows walking mindlessly in the same paths;

only because we have always done things the same way, never questioning ourselves."

In *JAMA* (*The Journal of the American Medical Association*) two years ago, spokespersons for Mount Sinai Medical Center in New York and the University of Washington School of Medicine explained that "A patient's unimproving health may lead the physician to feel guilty, insecure, frustrated and inadequate. Rather than address these feelings, the physicians may withdraw from patients." Some doctors may rationalize that their time can be better spent caring for the living. The result is that they and we decathect.

As much as I would like to think that the situation is very slowly getting better, and that we are eliminating bad deaths, I just do not see that happening. Maybe it will improve as more baby-boomers find themselves dealing with the failing health of their parents and demand better. I hope so. Yet presently not a week goes by that I do not hear from someone about the terrible death their friend or family member had to endure. Just today, as I write this, the widow of a dear friend of mine called. She told me about how one of my best friends, whom I had known since 1985, played tennis with many times, and whose friendship I greatly valued, died in agony yesterday. Despite being in hospice care, he suffered greatly for at least five hours, begging to be put out of his misery, before finally having the relief of dying. Damn, I hope we change this.

# What You Need to Know About Advance Directives and Advocacy

9

*To be prepared is half the victory.*
— Miguel de Cervantes

One of the most popular and well-received programs that I offer is about how to make advance directives work for you. In my three- or four-hour training sessions, we enact role playing, show a video demonstration, give about twenty-five pages of handout material, and inevitably bring many concerns and questions to the surface. This chapter covers some of the material from that course, including some wording you may wish to incorporate in your directives.

If you care to watch a video on the subject, we recorded one a little over sixteen years ago, demonstrating my advocacy for someone who wishes for medical treatment to be withheld. It was recorded by amateurs at a time when I was overweight, and it is probably longer than need be. Nevertheless, it still demonstrates how to advocate with power of attorney for health care for another person. It is at *www.youtube.com/watch?v=bfedGnAtJnI.*

An advance health care directive, also known as living will, personal directive, advance directive, or advance decision, is a document in which a person specifies which actions should be taken for their health care. These are usually, but not necessarily, written to come into effect when one is no longer able to make decisions for oneself because of illness or incapacity.

## Types of Advance Directives

- **Durable Health Care Power of Attorney.** This empowers someone else to make binding decisions for you.
- **Mental Health Power of Attorney.** This allows you to designate a trusted person (your "Agent") to make mental health care decisions on your behalf. When a doctor has determined you no longer have the capacity to make decisions for yourself, this document will go into effect.

- **Letter to my Agent.** You might explain your health care wishes again and why you chose this person.
- **Letter to my Doctor.** State what you do and do not want as medical treatment.
- **Living Will.** This generally directs health professionals to withdraw or withhold life-sustaining treatment if a patient is terminally ill or in a persistent vegetative state and can no longer communicate.
- **Do Not Resuscitate (DNR).** A DNR order pertains only to CPR. This is a medical order that requires health professionals not to intervene if a patient is found with no pulse or is not breathing. This sometimes goes by other names, including Prehospital Medical Care Directive and, in some institutions, the term I prefer: Allow Natural Death (AND).
- **Sectarian Health Care Directive.** This addendum to the advance directive clarifies your wish to be transferred to another facility if you are in an institution that will not honor your wishes because of religious policies.
- **Physician Orders for Life-Sustaining Treatment (POLST).** This is present in most states now, and it has some "teeth" because it is a doctor's order. It can follow you from home to nursing home to hospital. Other directives have little clout: they are merely an expression of your wishes. In a POLST, you can specify which interventions you in fact do not want, such as being on a respirator or receiving artificial hydration and nutrition. For information on POLST or similar programs in your state, check *http://polst.org/programs-in-your-state.*
- **Directions for Disposition of Body at Death.** All other Powers of Attorney are gone the minute you die, so this is important as a separate document. In many states, you can identify yourself as an organ donor on your driver's license. One reputable place to donate organs is the Life Legacy Foundation (*http://www.lifelegacy.org*). Or you may want to give your body to a local medical school for research and training — contact the school to determine whether it is in need of cadavers and what its terms are. Most offer free cremation. Another possible option is donating your body to a body farm to use for forensic research and training. A more comprehensive list of disposition options can be found in the book *Final Rights* by Lisa Carlson and Joshua Slocum.

Many years ago when End of Life Choices Arizona (now Final Exit Network) sold packets of advance directives at cost, a friend bought five packets. When I asked her why she needed five, she replied that her children were coming for a Thanksgiving dinner and she wanted to make sure they all had them. Yes! One need not be elderly to benefit from such protection. It would be good if every adult eighteen years of age or older had such documents, as well as an informed and competent advocate. After all, life is fragile and one never knows what unforeseen events might happen. In the famous cases of Terry Schiavo (where even the president of the United States got involved), Karen Ann Quinlan, and Nancy Cruzan, one might note well that these women were all in their twenties when they were rendered comatose. Another case covered prominently in the media was that of the courageous Brittany Maynard, who was only twenty-nine when she became terminally ill and ended her life in November of 2014.

> Life is a flickering candle we all carry around. A gust of wind, a meaningless accident, a microsecond of carelessness, and it's out. Forever.
>
> — David Wong, *John Dies at the End*

When I taught University Death Education in the 1970s, I found a paradox among my undergraduate students. On one hand, they exhibited genuine interest in the topic. On the other hand, the reality of personal mortality was rather remote. Many, if not most, college-age folk do not foresee death as an immediate possibility when applied to their own existence. One student typified this notion when each class member was asked to speculate about his or her own eventual demise. This fellow blithely told us that he would die at age 109, just after having dashed into a burning building to rescue six imperiled children. Sure!

## Begin by Assessing Your Values

The following are questions to consider as you make decisions and prepare documents concerning your health-care preferences. Use the questions as "food for thought" and discuss your wishes with your family, friends, and health-care providers.

- What will be important to you when you are dying (e.g., physical comforts, freedom from pain, the presence of family members)?
- How do you feel about the use of life-sustaining measures in the face of terminal illness? Permanent coma? Irreversible chronic illness, such as Alzheimer's disease, which is expected to reach 160 million people worldwide by 2050?

- Do you have strong feelings about particular medical procedures? Some procedures to think about include: mechanical breathing (respirator), cardiopulmonary resuscitation (CPR), artificial nutrition and hydration, hospital intensive care, pain relief medication, chemo or radiation therapy, and surgery.
- What limitations to your physical and mental health would affect the health-care decisions you would make? (Examples might include if you are paralyzed or if you are declared mentally incompetent.)
- Would you want to have financial matters taken into account when treatment decisions are made?
- Would you want to be placed in a nursing home if your condition warranted?
- Would you prefer hospice care, with the goal of keeping you comfortable in your home during the final period of your life, as an alternative to hospitalization?
- In general, do you wish to participate or share in making decisions about your health care and medical treatment?
- Would you always want to know the truth about your condition, treatment options, and the chance of recovery?

## What is Most Important to You?

Following is a list of preferences, some of which may compete with each other. In sorting out your own wishes, think about which of these are most important to you.

- Letting nature take its course
- Preserving quality of life
- Staying true to my spiritual beliefs/traditions
- Living as long as possible regardless of quality of life
- Being independent
- Being comfortable, and as pain-free as possible
- Leaving good memories for my family and friends
- Making a contribution to medical research or teaching
- Being able to relate to family and friends
- Being free of physical limitations
- Being mentally alert and competent
- Being able to leave money to family, friends, or charity

- Dying in a short while rather than lingering
- Avoiding expensive care

## Obstacles to Having Your Wishes Honored

Most of us will die some sort of managed death in a medical institution, such as a hospital, hospice, or nursing home. This means that someone will likely be making decisions about how you die. It is my conviction that the best-informed decisions to be made are your own.

A hundred years ago, before dramatic leaps in medical technology, most Americans died at home. Now, about eighty percent of people say they would prefer to die at home, but only about twenty percent do. We face a dilemma because not many want the burden of caring for a dying person. Dying at home is not easy. Death can be a relief not only to the one dying, but for the caregiver too. As my friend Renée says about caring for her difficult (ornery) and failing mother: "Oh dear God, please deliver her from my misery!"

> The good thing about death is it kills you once while life kills you for a lifetime. In fact death rescues you from life.
>
> — Bangambiki Habyarimana, *The Great Pearl of Wisdom*

Long ago I realized that human beings are quite capable of infinite perversity. We are all capable of doing something utterly mad. Although keeping someone alive against their wishes is not as monstrous as other cruel and heartless acts, doing so is nonetheless a perversity and I consider it to be simply opprobrious action of titanic proportions. It is regrettable and draconian that our medical technological advances of about the last fifty years have instilled a proclivity to do this, and even worse that our death-denying culture seems all too often to sanction doing so.

> In the natural course of events, the period when death is taking over a body is fairly brief. My grandfather (who had no medication) had about a fortnight of this period in his life. Today it can drag on for months or years.
>
> — Jennifer Worth, *In the Midst of Life*

Almost everyone eventually needs care from either a paid assistant or, more often, a relative — and the toll on that person can be enormous. The aide or family member is expected to bathe, dress and feed the dying person, to assist in the bathroom and to keep track of narcotics and other powerful medications, as well as doctor visits. Even loving, healthy people have trouble when they are thrust into this role for a family member or friend. It is harder for family members who are ill themselves, or resentful, overburdened, exhausted, and depressed.

There are many advantages to the old tradition of dying in the comfort of familiar surroundings, with friends and family nearby, and perhaps a pet at your side. This creates a clear understanding that death is near. (Again: most people who are terminally ill know it. Whether or not they choose to talk about it is another matter.) Ideally, with death at home, one is able to make necessary preparations with the assistance and support of loved ones.

But in practice, an orderly death is rare, as it generally comes with unpredictable timing from a predictably fatal chronic disease.

The appalling fact is that seventy to eighty percent of the time, our wishes will not be honored, even with a Living Will and other completed documents. Aside from completing all documents in an informed and thoughtful way, the critical factor is naming a strong advocate. More on that later, but it should be kept in mind in reviewing all of the related issues.

## Choosing the Right Words to Express Your Wishes

There is no need to start from scratch in putting end-of-life (and other medical care) wishes on paper. There are excellent books and other resources on the subject. One book I like is *To Die Well* by Sidney Wanzer, which includes appendixes with sample forms and language to use.

There is no legal assurance that caregivers will always honor all of your specific wishes, such as withholding fluids or administering sedation. However, including such specific requests will help to make it completely clear that the patient absolutely does not wish to live in a certain specified state such as dementia. Again, a strong advocate can help to make sure that your wishes get honored properly.

This can be a struggle. The Harvard School of Public Health recently reported that nearly one in three Medicare recipients underwent major surgery in the last year of life, one in five in the last month of life, one in ten in the last week of life. Yet nine in ten doctors say they would reject aggressive treatment at the end of their own lives.

Remember: you can modify the wording of state documents to meet your own personal criteria and needs. Sometimes, if a hospital staff person's beliefs are not in agreement with your advance directives, the reader/caregiver may feign deliberate confusion and adhere to his/her own interpretation. If your immediate caregiver is convinced that it is God's decree to keep you alive as long as possible, you're in trouble without a tough advocate overseeing your care every step of the way!

English doctors tell a joke about this imperative: "Why in Ireland do they put screws in coffins? To keep the doctors out." I have a cartoon depicting a patient lying in a hospital bed with multiple tubes and intravenous connections, with the doctor standing in a minatory way next to the bed saying, "Medical ethics do not allow me to assist in your death. I am, however, permitted to keep you miserable as long as possible."

This has become the American way of dying — agonized and prolonged imprisonment in an intensive care unit, pinned down under a maze of tubes and machines, enduring one medical procedure after another, unable to hold or be held by loved ones. You will have a better chance of countering resistance to your wishes if you add language such as the following to your advance directive:

> In the event that there needs to be an exercise of judgment in areas of this directive which seem vague due to particular circumstances, I wish the judgment to err on the side of death rather than prolongation of life.
>
> My attorney or my surrogate (agent, proxy) has the authority to completely override what would appear to others to be the clear meaning and intent of anything in this document. His/her exercise of the authority so stated exempts him from any harm based on his decisions.
>
> Such circumstances are not restricted to the final stages of a terminal disease but should encompass an illness (terminal or not) when death is not necessarily imminent. When the issues of health care and comfort versus pain dominate my view of a future that offers little or no hope or respite, my Power of Attorney's decision is tantamount to my own decision.

Also note that the words, "when I cannot make my own healthcare decisions" can be confusing because it is difficult to know with certainty when you reach that point. The words you and your advocate will hear people saying are "capacity" or "decision-making capacity." When you hear these words, someone is questioning whether or not you can make your own decisions or if it is time for your advocate to make your decisions. The determination of "capacity" is difficult because it changes from person to person, depending on the circumstances.

If you really trust your advocate, you may want to look closely at the standard paragraphs that defer the rights of Durable Power of Attorney until you are unable to make your own healthcare decisions. You may want to change the wording to make your Durable Power of Attorney document effective immediately or at another specific time.

## SAMPLE LANGUAGE

The following is sample language that can be used to reinforce the ability of your advocate or agent to make decisions on your behalf. Naturally, the language can be altered to reflect your specific desires:

My agent knows my goals and wishes based on our conversations and on any other guidance I might have written. My agent has full authority to make decisions for me about my healthcare according to my goals and wishes. If the choice I would make is unclear, then my agent will decide based on what he or she believes to be in my best interests. My agent's authority to interpret my wishes is intended to be as broad as possible, and includes the following authority:

1. To agree to, refuse, or withdraw consent to any type of medical care, treatment, surgical procedures, tests, or medications. This includes decisions about using mechanical or other procedures that affect any bodily function, such as artificial respiration, artificially supplied nutrition and hydration (that is, tube feeding), cardiopulmonary resuscitation, or other forms of medical support, even if deciding to stop or withhold treatment could or would result in my death;

2. To have access to medical records and information to the same extent that I am entitled to, including the right to disclose health information to others;

3. To authorize my admission to or discharge (even against medical advice) from any hospital, nursing home, residential care, assisted-living or similar facility or service;

4. To contract for any health-related service or facility for me, or apply for public or private health care benefits, with the understanding that my agent is not personally financially responsible for those contracts;

5. To hire and fire medical, social service, and other support personnel who are responsible for my care;

6. To authorize my participation in medical research related to my medical condition;

7. To agree to or refuse using any medication or procedure intended to relieve pain or discomfort, even though that use may lead to physical damage or dependence or hasten (but not intentionally cause) my death;

8. To decide about organ and tissue donations, autopsy, and the disposition of my remains as the law permits;

9. To take any other action necessary to do what I authorize here, including signing waivers or other documents, pursuing any dispute resolution process, or taking legal action in my name.

> Health care providers can rely on my agent. No one who relies in good faith on any representations by my agent or back-up agent will be liable to me, my estate, my heirs or assigns, for recognizing the agent's authority. I cancel any previous power of attorney for health care that I may have signed. I intend this power of attorney to be universal; it is valid in any jurisdiction in which it is presented. I intend that copies of this document are as effective as the original. My agent will not be entitled to compensation for services performed under this power of attorney, but he or she will be entitled to reimbursement for all reasonable expenses that result from carrying out any provision of this power of attorney.

## ADDITIONAL CONSIDERATIONS

> There is absolutely no worse death curse than the humdrum daily existence of the living dead.
>
> — Anthon St. Maarten

The keys to dying well are to know what you want and do not want when nearing death, putting those preferences in writing, and communicating those preferences to your advocate, doctor, and family members. As discussed in the previous chapter, a person near the end of life almost always needs the help of an advocate in order to have his/her medical wishes honored.

At the risk of repetition, your advocate may go by a different title in some states — the person may be referred to legally as a "proxy," "agent," "surrogate," or similar term. Needless to say, an advocate with legally binding power of attorney for your health care must be someone very familiar with your wishes. You should also keep in mind that all directives are state-specific. A physician in another state might honor your out-of-state directive, but may not be legally required to do so.

If you reside in two states or frequently travel to another state, it is important to fill out the appropriate forms for each state. You can do so by searching the Internet for "advance directives (name of state)," and proceed from there. Or you might call the office of your state's Attorney General or Secretary of State to get the necessary forms.

As noted earlier, most directives are worded so that they do not go into effect until you are unable to speak for yourself, but you can change that to make them effective now or any time you specify.

Despite laws requiring hospitals to make advance directives available to patients, end-of-life wishes are routinely ignored. Why? Because far too many doctors and hospitals equate death with failure. Death is disguised. Even though most of us die in a hospital, you are unlikely to see it there. The deceased are transported in stretchers with false bottoms. That apparently vacant stretcher next to you in the elevator may not really be empty.

For reasons of culture, personal religious beliefs, arrogance, or fear of a lawsuit, medical personnel instinctively act to delay death as long as possible, even when the patient protests. And there is another factor that plays into the failure to respect advance directives: money. Reimbursement policies promote expensive tests and procedures, some of which are invasive and invidious, and which are often counter to patients' wishes.

About twenty years ago I wrote a bit of poetry about the state of those terminally ill among us, who are subject to and vulnerable to the will of others. They are:

dehumanized and marginalized,
drugged and plugged,
medicalized and bureaucratized,
under appreciated, needlessly emaciated and overly sedated,
alive but deprived,
isolated and denigrated,
neglected and rejected,
and sometimes even adroitly exploited.

## Gaining a Better Understanding of Advance Directives

Following are answers to some commonly asked questions:

**Q.** What is the proper term for the appointment of a person who can speak on a patient's behalf?

**A.** Spokespersons for patients are referred to by various names, depending on the state in which they live. Examples include "health care power of attorney," "health care proxy," "surrogate," and "agent."

**Q.** Must an advance directive name a patient spokesperson?

**A.** Some advance directives identify a person to speak on a patient's behalf, but the provision is not required.

**Q.** When does a living will take effect?

**A.** The majority of living wills say not to treat a patient after the patient has entered into a terminal condition, despite sound medical treatment, or if the patient remains in a permanently unconscious state. A living will can be written to accept or refuse specific lifesaving medical care during such an event, including mechanical respiration, antibiotics, or insertion of a feeding tube.

**Q.** What is necessary for a health-care power of attorney to begin making health care choices for the patient?

**A.** The necessary requirements for a power of attorney to be activated depend on the jurisdiction. However, many states say two physicians first must determine that a patient is unable to communicate and direct his or her own medical care.

**Q.** When is an advance directive enacted?

**A.** Advance directives are activated based on the details within the document. The directive's language should be read closely to be sure the patient's circumstances call for the order to become triggered and then followed.

## What Does Your Advocate Need to Know about Your Health?

Your advocate will be able to represent you with confidence if you include him or her in discussions about your health status starting now. When you experience a serious illness, your advocate will be better prepared to speak for you if he or she knows your medical history as well as what is new or of immediate concern. You and your advocate might ask the following questions of your health-care providers based on the most current health information that is available:

1. What is your diagnosis (disease or illness) in terms you and your advocate can understand?
2. What is your prognosis (course of the illness) in the short-term and the long-term? Is it certain or untenable?
3. Considering the diagnosis and the prognosis, what is the "best case" and what is the "worst case" that you will experience?
4. What are your health-care providers trying to achieve for you (goals of care)?
5. What are the treatment options, and how will they affect your prognosis? (Better? Worse?)
6. What does your health-care provider recommend be done next?
7. If you decide to do nothing, what will happen next?

Don't settle for statistics — ask how treatment options will affect your well-being and your day-to-day life. You will want to consider a number of factors that may help or hinder the process of making advocacy decisions.

Possibly helpful are: the advocate's characteristics and life experiences; good coping strategies; religious community support; spiritual beliefs; the advocate's social network; support from family and friends; working toward consensus; knowing full well your wishes and preferences; being readily available; forthright recommendations from the care provider; and respect from the care provider.

Factors that may hinder the process are: too many care providers involved; not knowing who is in charge; confusion about your preferences for medical care; being overcome by emotion; family conflicts; competing responsibilities; financial barriers; and the advocate's own health problems.

## Questions You or Your Advocate Might Ask Your Doctor

Begin with letting your doctor know that you want "the truth, the whole truth, and nothing but the truth."

Commonly, doctors have only a few minutes to speak with you. If you have ailments, it is best to arrive with a list of written questions to be sure they are addressed and answered in plain English, not medical jargon. The following questions were compiled by Ms. Tani Bahti, RN, CT, CHPN, a fellow thanatologist in Tucson.

- What is the diagnosis and what is your prognosis?
- Is the goal of this treatment to cure, prolong life, or relieve symptoms?
- What is the best I can hope for with this treatment?
- What is the worst I should prepare for if this doesn't work?
- Is this a standard treatment or experimental?
- What are the chances for success in my particular case?
- How and when will I know it's working?
- How will this impact my daily living, comfort and/or goals?
- What are the physical changes I may experience and how will you help me manage them?
- Will I need extra help to manage at home, and if so, for how long?
- What are the side effects? If I have side effects, how long might they last?
- What can be done to prevent or minimize them?
- Are there any potentially permanent side effects?
- Is this covered under my insurance?

- What will the cost be to me?
- If I refuse this treatment, what can I expect to happen?
- Are there other ways to manage my disease and would you recommend them? Why or why not?
- What might be some other options?
- If I refuse this treatment, will you still be my doctor?
- Is there a counselor, support group, or someone I can talk to about this?
- Do you have material about this treatment that I can take home and review?

## Questions You Might Ask Yourself

The following questions, also compiled by Tani Bahti, can help you to make a clear decision.

- Do I have all the information I need to make an informed decision? (Major decisions are often made on the basis of insufficient information.)
- Of what am I most afraid?
- Is fear or lack of information pushing me toward a particular decision?
- What are my goals at this time in my life and will this treatment help me reach those goals?
- Am I making this decision based on what I believe someone else wants or is this what I really/truly want?
- If someone else: Have I discussed and clarified with that person what each of us wants?
- Who/What is my source of strength and support and have I used it?
- If I have a terminal illness, how do I want to spend the time I have?
- Have I put my affairs in order, said my goodbyes, taken care of any unfinished business — emotional and pragmatic?
- What does "fighting the good fight" mean to me?
- Does it involve seeking aggressive treatment until the end or allowing a natural death?
- Have I completed all advance directives, and do I have someone empowered with medical power of attorney — an advocate or surrogate?
- Have I discussed the directives with my doctor and family?

- Have I asked all of my questions, expressed my fears and concerns, and shared what I really feel with my family, friends, and physician?

## Keeping Your Advocate Involved

In many of my PowerPoint presentations I show a cartoon of a man seated on a hospital bed wearing only a skimpy hospital gown and the caption reads, "Medical studies indicate that most people suffer a sixty-eight percent hearing loss when naked."

The point I make is that it is important to have your advocate with you when visiting the doctor. Not only can that person help you ask the right questions and get the answers in plain English, but they can also help you absorb the information.

For example, if the doctor says something like, "Well, Joe, we have run all the tests and I am sorry to have to tell you that you do have cancer. In fact, it is a particularly virulent form of cancer." Then the doctor proceeds to explain that the medical community can or cannot do this or that. In all likelihood, Joe has not heard a damn thing after hearing his diagnosis of a virulent form of cancer.

## Tips on Getting Your Wishes Honored

> As for dying, we can only assay that once; we are all apprentices when it comes to that.
>
> — Michel de Montaigne, *The Complete Essays*

At the risk of redundancy, I will emphasize again that it is critical to have an advocate, and to the extent possible, that person should accompany you whenever you encounter any medical institution/caregiver.

And again, remember that all advance directives are state-specific. Another state may honor your wishes as expressed in your home state, but may not be required to do so. There is a national registry for advance directives, and some states have their own state registries. You may use the Internet to find the appropriate document for your state, or find the national registry at *https://www.uslivingwillregistry.com*.

"Talk about what things make life worth living for you," advises Dr. Rebecca Aslakson from Johns Hopkins Hospital. "People feel reassured, even downright virtuous, when they have completed their paperwork, but if the family doesn't know about it, if the medical team doesn't know about it, it might as well not exist."

One always, and everywhere, has the right to say "no." Legal precedents leading to modern views of end-of-life issues date back to an 1891 Supreme

Court ruling that people should have control over their own bodies. From that precedent grew an understanding that a person must understand and agree to medical treatment and that a right of informed consent does not end when one becomes incapacitated. You have a right to refuse treatment. This includes the right to leave the hospital if, for example, one would rather die at home in familiar surroundings with loved ones present. You may have to sign a waiver stating that your decision to leave is against the advice of the hospital, but you can leave nevertheless.

Even if you choose to stay in the hospital, you may still have a limited right to refuse medical treatment. That right of refusal is limited because it has to be balanced with other objectives of the hospital, such as preventing suicide, protecting third parties such as children, protecting the ethical integrity of doctors, and the hospital's mission to preserve life when possible.

## Know the Views of Your Caregivers

Much depends upon the attitude of your immediate primary caregiver.

My father, a quiet and soft-spoken gentleman who largely just said what he meant and meant what he said, was the executive director of a hospital. One evening at the dinner table, when I was home from college, he explained: "You know, I don't run the hospital. The board of directors doesn't run the hospital. The doctors may think they do, but they don't run the hospital. The nurses run the hospital." It is the hands-on, day-in and day-out, immediate quality of care that makes the most difference.

There is some scant research on directives not honored. When given hypothetical situations involving imaginary patients with living wills, nearly two-thirds of 117 doctors surveyed said they would not follow the orders. They were most likely to diverge from the documents when confronted with family members with differing views, or when there was a hopeful prognosis for the patient.

"There are two obvious reasons why a doctor might not follow an advance directive," said Dr. Howard Brody, a bioethicist at Michigan State University. "Reason one is that the doctor is a jerk and is practicing unethical medicine. The second reason is that the advance directive is unfollowable." In other words, the language may be too vague, with terms like "no heroics," which would be subject to interpretation, and most physicians will err on the side of trying to keep you alive.

Other factors can include profit motive, religious bias, threat of litigation, carelessness, mistakes, incompetence, and the training of medical staff to sustain life and consider death to be a failure. Again, much boils down to the attitude of your primary caregiver.

## Keeping Your Advance Directive Current

Many studies over the last decade suggest that advance directives, especially Living Wills, are not particularly helpful. Why? The problem, according to Alan Meisel, a professor of law and bioethics at the University of Pittsburgh, is that it's impossible for people to fine-tune in advance what they do — and do not — want in the way of medical care. We never know what the situation will be, as it is often complex and constantly changing.

Store your advance directives in all relevant places and maintain a record of where the original documents and the copies are filed and when they were given to each individual.

Review the document periodically — ideally every six months to a year — in case you change your mind, or new procedures are developed or new situations arise, and sign or initial and date any revisions, thus showing consistent, rational wishes. The American Bar Association Commission on Law and Aging suggests that you re-examine your health care wishes whenever any of the following "five D's" occurs:

- Decade: When you start each new decade of your life.
- Death: When you experience the death of a loved one.
- Divorce: When you experience a divorce or other major family change. (In many states, a divorce automatically revokes the authority of a spouse who had been named as agent.)
- Diagnosis: When you are diagnosed with a serious medical problem.
- Decline: When you experience a significant decline or deterioration from an existing health condition, especially when it diminishes your ability to live independently.

Have copies of the documents handy, storing them in multiple personal sites: in a home safe, on the refrigerator, in the car glove compartment, in your purse, online, etc. Your advocate gets an original, and you keep an original, perhaps signed in blue or red ink so as to stand out as original.

Be sure to give copies to key family members and close friends as well as your primary care doctor. If entering a hospital, give a copy to the official hospital advocate. It may be helpful to also give a copy to your personal attorney, preferably one familiar with elder law.

Obtain a copy of the "Patients' Rights" statement from any medical institution providing care, study this document carefully, and provide copies to people who also have your advanced directives.

Documents can be witnessed or notarized. Do both. Usually there is no need to use an attorney to fill out these documents, but again, if you have a personal attorney who is knowledgeable about elder law or estate planning, a legal review may be a good idea.

Do not put the document in a safe deposit box or with your will, as access would come too late.

## Qualifications of an Advocate

It is best if your advocate:

- Is legally qualified with durable power of attorney for health care. (See the listing below for factors that would disqualify a person.)
- Is thoroughly familiar with your wishes: your physical, emotional, financial, and spiritual state. Choose someone who will talk with you now about your wishes, who will understand what you want and your priorities about health care, and who will faithfully do as you ask or have previously stated when the time comes. Communicate often and give specifics about every six months.
- Lives near you or could easily travel to be with you quickly in an emergency situation. If your primary preference is someone who lives far away, a local person could be appointed to serve temporarily until your primary advocate is able to arrive.
- Is introduced to others involved with your care.
- Has original documents signed in blue or red ink.
- Can handle conflicting opinions from family members, friends, and medical personnel. Disagreement among family members is not uncommon.
- Is not a relative, yet someone with whom you implicitly trust as a true confidant.
- Has people skills, a prepossessing demeanor, and plenty of bonhomie with an indomitable perseverance.
- Is articulate, assertive, and indefatigable, as having your wishes honored can be quite a struggle.
- Is able to refuse useless medical efforts, exhibit moxie and equanimity when under stress, and not capitulate when confronted with medical staff's reluctance or objections to having one's wishes honored. Your advocate must be strong enough to overcome the possible unresponsiveness of a doctor or medical institution.
- Can be a "son-of-a-bitch" or "witch-on-wheels" if need be. It can be quite an uphill struggle to make sure you get what you want, and to not get what you do not want from medical treatment. Sometimes

your advocate must be adamantine, hidebound, and well able to fulminate beyond risking a mere peccadillo.
- Is someone with whom you have an inviolable trust. Probity is critical. After all, these are literally life-or-death decisions.

## WHOM NOT TO CHOOSE AS YOUR ADVOCATE

I suggested above that you consider appointing someone other than a close relative for several reasons. Not that your friends do not love you too, but a friend may be able to be a bit more objective in honoring your wishes. For example, I know three women in Tucson who had served as advocate for their respective mothers. Although they faithfully followed the mother's wishes by withholding various procedures and treatments, these loving daughters still feel guilty about having been complicitous in their mothers' deaths. This is inappropriate guilt, but still haunting them to this day.

A spouse may find it very difficult to let one's beloved partner die. And there is a chance that an immediate relative who is not so loving may have the ulterior motive of standing to gain financially by hastening the death.

You will need to choose someone who meets the legal requirements to act as a health care agent. State requirements differ, but to meet the combined requirements of every state, your health care agent should be an adult who is of sound mind, and not anyone in the following list:

- Your health care providers or the owner or operator of a health or residential care facility that is currently serving you.
- A spouse, employee, or spouse of an employee of your health care providers.
- Anyone who professionally evaluates your capacity to make decisions.
- Anyone who works for a government agency that is financially responsible for your care (unless that person is a blood relative).
- Anyone that a court has already appointed to be your guardian or conservator.
- Anyone who already serves as a health care agent for ten or more people.

One may have only one advocate with health-care power of attorney at one time, but you can appoint a secondary or tertiary person. If, for example, your primary person lives out of state, you could have someone local serve in this role temporarily until your primary person arrives.

Medical records belong to you. You or your advocate must insist that all advance directive documents be put at the very top of your medical chart daily. Do so even with electronic files. This keeps caregivers aware of your wishes and helps avoid having your wishes buried and forgotten.

There is recourse available if one's wishes are not being followed, such as taking the case to the hospital advocate, the hospital administrator, the hospital's ethics committee, or going to court. Court is a last resort, but even with our log-jammed legal system, you or your advocate can get in front of a judge within 2–48 hours in a life-or-death matter, such as being disconnected from a ventilator.

If wishes are not honored, you (or your estate) may also be able to sue for negligence, malpractice, recklessness, fraud, oppression, etc., but that is usually after you are dead.

If things are not going well, I even go so far as to advise people to tell a fib if they have to as a last resort: "My son-in-law, a medical malpractice attorney, is beginning to get quite concerned. . . ." Regardless of whether you even have a son-in-law, it gets the medical staff's attention because doctors are so afraid of being sued. Doctors often practice defensive medicine, running all kinds of tests and procedures just to protect themselves.

All too often, medical care is confused with love. They're not the same thing. Sometimes the best thing you can do for someone you love is to stop the medical care.

Of course, there are those who oppose the right to die. And that is fine: nothing wrong with holding a different point of view. If one chooses to rage against death to the grave, wanting everything possible done to preserve life, that's their prerogative. Just do not try to impose your beliefs on me. As Viktor Frankl said, "Being tolerant does not mean that I share another's belief. But it does mean that I acknowledge another's right to believe and obey his own conscience."

Frequently, family members disagree about which procedures and treatment should be administered or withheld. This has come up often in my presence, with some family members wanting to keep the patient alive no matter what, even though such a desire is expressly against the wishes stated by the patient.

I wish I had a more compassionate answer to this problem, but here is the best advice I can offer: if you have family members who disagree with your wishes, just do not include them. You might try to win them over, but they may not change their minds. Familial objections can present great difficulty because doctors are afraid of being sued, so don't even let them know you are in the hospital! A surviving friend or family member can still invite them to to your funeral. Such familial objections can present great difficulty because doctors are so afraid of being sued, and the person objecting will still be alive to sue. What one wishes for oneself may not be the same as what one wishes for another person, and *vice versa*.

# ACTIVE DYING 10

*Where were the scientific pamphlets that taught a woman how to listen to herself die?*

— Gail Carriger, *Heartless*

MOST OF US ARE UNABLE to recognize when someone is close to death. This chapter will help you to spot the clues.

Even if scientists cannot say for sure what is going on inside a dying person's head and body, or why, they do tend to know how the last hours look. With the exception of those who die unexpectedly — from trauma, heart attack or stroke — dying has many familiar hallmarks.

Imagine that the person dying is you. This is something that is all but impossible to do; even in dreams we usually force ourselves awake before the last, fatal moment. But it's an interesting exercise, so try to picture it. You've been in hospice care for, say, three weeks, and caregivers have been coming to your home twice a week to take your pulse, listen to your heart, and talk about how to treat your pain and constipation. Today the doctor tells your caretaker that you may have only a few days left to live.

Your hands and feet are cold to the touch. You twitch occasionally. Your face is drawn, your lips are dry, and you do not get out of bed even to use the bathroom. Using the bathroom is irrelevant by now anyway; you have not eaten anything for days, so your urinary and digestive tracts have mostly shut down. Slowly, though you cannot necessarily feel it, all of your other organs are shutting down too.

If you could see yourself, you would see that your lips look blue. Your hands and feet might be blue as well. You breathe rapidly, except for the long stretches of time when you do not really seem to breathe at all.

You spend your time in a kind of limbo between waking and sleeping. You know who you are and where you are, yet you are seeing visions. Those relatives who have been dead for years appear and disappear at your bedside. You want to tell them something, but you do not talk to them, nor do you mention them to your caretaker. Indeed, you do not talk much to anyone, imaginary or real.

Sometimes you moan, but you are probably in no distress; that's just what happens when your throat muscles go flaccid. Toward the end, your jaw moves up and down with every breath, almost as if you were chewing something. And as you breathe, you make an eerie sound. That is the death rattle; you are not coming back.

In the mid 1970s my friend Peter witnessed the death of his mother. As she was dying, she exhibited the death rattle. This is known clinically as terminal respiratory secretions or simply terminal secretions. It is a sound often produced by someone who is near death when fluids such as saliva and bronchial secretions accumulate in the throat and upper chest. Those who are dying may lose their ability to swallow and may have increased production of bronchial secretions, resulting in such an accumulation. Peter found this sound so unsettling that he had to leave her room. He fled in fright. Although the death rattle can appear to be quite discomforting and it may seem to be painful to the dying person, my understanding is that it is not painful and the dying person is not suffering. It is merely a biological reflex.

The scariest part about dying, at least to me, is how it ends: with the immutable fact of no longer existing. Ever! But there are other common fears: dying alone and dying in pain and suffering. Today, say specialists in end-of-life care, no one has to do either.

Two phases lead up to the actual time of death: the "pre-active phase of dying" and the "active phase of dying." On average, the pre-active phase of dying may last approximately two weeks, while on average, the active phase of dying lasts about three days.

I say "on average" because there are always exceptions to the rule. Some people exhibit signs of pre-active dying for a month or longer, while others exhibit signs of the active phase of dying for two weeks. Many hospice staff have been fooled into thinking that death was about to occur when their patient had unusually low blood pressure or longer periods of pausing in the breathing rhythm. Some people with these symptoms, however, can suddenly recover and live a week, a month, or even longer. Low blood pressure alone or long pauses in breathing (apnea) are not reliable indicators of imminent death in all cases. God alone knows for sure when death will occur.

## Signs of the Pre-Active Phase of Dying

- Increased restlessness, confusion, agitation, inability to stay content in one position and insisting on changing positions frequently (exhausting family and caregivers)
- Withdrawal from active participation in social activities
- Pain, which may show as grimaces, groans, or scowls, and should be managed

- Increased periods of sleep, lethargy
- Decreased intake of food and liquids
- Periods of pausing in the breathing (apnea) whether awake or sleeping
- Reports seeing persons who had already died
- States that he or she is dying
- Requests family visit to settle "unfinished business" and tie up "loose ends"
- Inability to heal or recover from wounds or infections
- Increased swelling (edema) of either the extremities or the entire body

## SIGNS OF THE ACTIVE PHASE OF DYING

- Inability to arouse the dying person at all (coma), or ability to arouse only with great effort but then having the person quickly return to an unresponsive state (semi-coma)
- Severe agitation, hallucinations, acting 'crazy' and not in the dying person's normal manner or personality
- Much longer periods of pausing in the breathing (apnea)
- Dramatic changes in the breathing pattern including apnea, but also including very rapid breathing or cyclic changes in the patterns of breathing (such as slow progressing to very fast and then slow again, or shallow progressing to very deep breathing while also changing rate of breathing to very fast and then slow)
- Other very abnormal breathing patterns
- Eyes may tear or become glazed
- Severe increase of respiratory congestion or fluid buildup in lungs
- Inability to swallow any fluids at all (not taking any food by mouth voluntarily as well)
- The dying person states that he or she is going to die
- The dying person is breathing through wide open mouth continuously and no longer can speak, even if awake
- Urinary or bowel incontinence in someone who was not incontinent before
- Marked decrease in urine output and darkening color of urine or very abnormal colors (such as red or brown)
- Blood pressure dropping dramatically from one's normal blood pressure range (more than a 20-point drop)

- Systolic blood pressure below seventy, diastolic blood pressure below fifty
- Extremities (such as hands, arms, feet and legs) feel very cold to the touch
- Complains that his or her legs or feet are numb and cannot be felt at all
- Cyanosis, or a bluish or purple coloring to the patient's arms and legs, especially the feet and hands
- The patient's body is held in rigid unchanging position
- Jaw drop; the patient's jaw is no longer held straight and may drop to the side
- A fairly sure sign that one is very close to death: the ear lobes lie flat against one's face

Although not all patients show all of these signs, many of these signs will be seen in some patients. The reason for the tradition of "keeping a vigil" when someone is dying is that we really do not know exactly when death will occur until it is obviously happening. If you wish to be there with your loved one when death occurs, keeping a vigil at the bedside is part of the process. When working with a hospice in Prescott, Arizona, I initiated a vigiling program. Now such programs exist in many hospices, usually staffed by volunteers.

In the lingering moments before you die, your body releases DMT. This is the drug that makes you dream, and this same drug is found in every living animal. It is not an evolutionary trick to make you survive. Your body is choosing to release this drug now because it believes your fate is too grim for you to comprehend. So you dream. You dream that everything will be fine. You dream that nothing happened at all. It is in this moment that your body sits across from you, much like an out-of-body experience. It tells you that it looks like we're not gonna make it this time. You sit around a fire and recollect the past before soon parting ways back to the atomic ether. Your body does this because it loves you. You have never met anyone like your body. Your body has been with you every day, good and bad. It has even kept a journal of your life carved in scars. Your eyelashes always wiped the tears from your eyes.

Always remember that the dying person can often hear others up until the very end, even though he or she cannot respond. Your presence at the bedside can be a great expression of your love, helping to the person to feel calmer and more at peace at the time of death.

If you have questions about any of the changing signs or symptoms appearing in your loved one, ask your doctor or nurse to explain them to you.

Regrettably, suffering is sometimes not abated and all too real. In her book *Before I Die*, Jenny Downham writes the following dialogue about one who is suffering:

> "I don't give a shit, Dad!"
>
> "Well I do! I absolutely give a shit! This will completely exhaust you."
>
> "It's my body. I can do what I like!"
>
> "So you don't care about your body now?"
>
> "No, I'm sick of it! I'm sick of doctors and needles and blood tests and transfusions. I'm sick of being stuck in a bed day after day while the rest of you get on with your lives. I hate it! I hate all of you! Adam's gone for a university interview, did you know that? He's going to be here for years doing whatever he likes and I'm going to be under the ground in a couple of weeks!"

Having witnessed human suffering all too often, I happen to believe in what I call "misery without compensation." In other words, not every cloud has a silver lining, and not everything works out for the best. Sometimes abject misery is just plain awful. As Auliq Ice said, "Deep down a broken heart, all the sadness one can bear is misery." Nora Ephron, in *I Remember Nothing: and Other Reflections*, put it this way:

> Everybody dies. There's nothing you can do about it. Whether or not you eat six almonds a day. Whether or not you believe in God. (Although there's no question a belief in God would come in handy. It would be great to think there's a plan, and that everything happens for a reason. I don't happen to believe that. And every time one of my friends says to me, "Everything happens for a reason," I would like to smack her.)

# Deliberate Life Completion 11
## The Best Option For Many

*I touch you knowing we weren't born tomorrow,*
*and somehow, each of us will help the other live,*
*and somewhere, each of us must help the other die.*
— Adrienne Rich, *Twenty One Love Poems*

Final Exit Network is the organization with which I work most closely, volunteering as its Arizona Affiliate Leader.

Because one can qualify for Final Exit Network services without necessarily being terminally ill, the Network is my favorite among several right-to-die organizations in this country. Another reason I favor Final Exit Network is because of its use of financial resources: It is almost entirely a volunteer operation. There are only a couple of part-time staff who work from their homes. FEN has no offices, high salaries, or other such overhead. The resources are used to actually support those seeking information and education about hastening death.

While never encouraging anyone to hasten their death, FEN maintains that anyone who is suffering intolerably should have a right to a peaceful, dignified, effective means of terminating the suffering. The Network's Exit Guide volunteers provide information, education, companionship, and emotional support to carefully screened candidates.

They do not provide any tangible physical assistance in death. They do not provide the means. If asked to do so, they sit with the person at the time of death because they believe nobody should ever have to die alone. I believe that to make a difference in someone's life you do not need to be rich, wise, beautiful or famous. You just have to be there when they need you.

The self-help guru Leo Buscaglia was once asked to help judge a contest to find the most caring child. The winner was a four-year-old boy whose next-door neighbor was an elderly gentleman who had recently lost his wife. Upon seeing the man crying on his porch, the little boy went into the old gentleman's yard, climbed onto his lap in the rocking chair, and just sat there. Upon his return home, when his mother asked the child what he had said to the neighbor, the little boy replied, "Nothing, I just helped him cry." Such compassionate presence reminds me of one of my favorite sayings: "Don't just do something, stand there!"

Contrary to popular belief, most of those who do in fact choose to end their suffering do not do so because of physical pain. These days, physical pain can be managed effectively about ninety-five percent of the time. Mind you, if you are one whose pain persists, it can be devastating. And the fear of recurring pain is as disabling as the pain itself. A good friend of mine, Doug, had the misfortune of having his daughter die from cancer while still in her twenties. One day while in the hospital, he moved to sit on her bed to comfort her. With seven pillows between him and her, she still screamed out in pain!

In states with physician aid in dying (PAD), only five percent of those who ended their lives did so because of physical pain. The three most frequently mentioned end-of-life concerns are: loss of autonomy (93%), decreasing ability to participate in activities that make life enjoyable (92%), and loss of dignity (78%).

## Many Varieties of Suffering

There are many varieties of existential suffering that could lead one to the radical decision to hasten death. These include: fear of or actual abandonment, other fears, anticipatory grief, anxiety, confusion, delirium, dependence on others, becoming a burden, clinical depression, feelings of futility, hopelessness, loneliness, loss of dignity or worth, psychic pain, extreme weariness (filled with lassitude and perhaps feeling desiccated), and more issues that may accompany the dying process.

For some, financial concerns play a role in the decision, though this is rarely the primary reason. Many would rather leave some assets to their children or their favorite charity than take on the expenses incurred with how we die these days. Many people spend more on health care in the last six months of life than in their whole life up to that point. And medical costs are the leading cause of bankruptcy, even for those with health insurance. In 2014 Medicare spent $50 billion(!) caring for people within the last three months of their lives. I am sure some of this was very helpful, but most of this enormous expenditure did little or nothing to prolong or improve people's lives.

For the right to die, requiring that one must be terminally ill is a severe restriction and prohibits PAD (Physician Aid in Dying) from going far enough. By including this criterion, PAD laws exclude many who may wish to hasten their deaths due to hopeless and interminable suffering experienced far in advance of being labeled "terminal," such as those with early-stage Alzheimer's Disease, progressive disorders such as ALS or MS, and much more. Those with dementia may have to wait until it is too late, being judged as incompetent to give informed consent for PAD.

Moreover, the term "terminal" is not always justly applied. I have a friend whose mother in a nursing home experienced enormous suffering and withered away to only fifty-eight pounds. Yet the doctors refused to declare that she was "terminal." It would be best if we were to terminate "terminal"!

Those who are not yet terminally ill and seek out the services of Final Exit Network include people suffering from debilitating diseases such as cancer, neurological diseases such as ALS (Lou Gehrig's disease), Alzheimer's, CTE (chronic traumatic encephalopathy), Parkinson's, Huntington's, and motor neuron diseases such as MS (multiple sclerosis) and muscular dystrophy, respiratory illnesses such as emphysema, degenerative afflictions such as congestive heart failure, stroke, AIDS (acquired immune deficiency syndrome, Addison's disease, Creutzfeltd-Jakob (mad cow disease), Guillain-Barre Syndrome, frontotemporal dementia, frontotemporal lobar degeneration, and others.

Additional afflictions that lead one to considering hastening one's death are Stevens-Johnson Syndrome, Ehlers-Danlos Syndrome (EDS), Tumer Parsonage Syndrome, demyelinating disease, complex regional pain syndrome (CRPS) Type I (formerly known as RSDS) and Type II (once known as causalgia).

People with neurodegenerative diseases such as ALS or Huntington's can suffer for years. Even being tired of life in old age can sometimes qualify one to receive the services of Exit Guides. There is pain that no medication can touch, like deep-bone pain from cancer or trigeminal nerve pain in the face. There are people who can no longer function or care for themselves, and they are terrified of the suffering that lies ahead of them. In most of these cases, Final Exit Network is the only organization available to help; the suffering patient is likely to be turned away by other right-to-die organizations.

It is regrettable that there is not more cooperation among the few right-to-die groups in this country. Recently I attended what was publicized as "a community conversation on medical aid in dying" in Tucson with about 200 people present. The local leader of Compassion and Choices (C&C, of which I am a lifetime member) actually tried to have me removed from the premises because I was telling people about Final Exit Network (FEN). She failed, and I did not leave. Because I was wearing a small FEN lapel pin on my blazer, a television reporter in attendance asked me about our organization, so I gave her a FEN membership brochure. As I was speaking with the reporter, the C&C leader rushed over, angrily exclaimed, "That is not our group," snatched the brochure out of the reporter's hand, and threw it into the nearby trash can. Such hostile antagonism certainly does not serve to further our cause nor have at heart those needlessly suffering near life's end who need our support.

I might add that Final Exit Network invites its members to participate in choosing who will represent them on the board of directors. The Network is the only U.S. right-to-die membership organization with open elections for board members. Having attended several meetings of this board of directors, I would be hard-pressed to cite an equally compassionate, competent, and committed group of people.

Sure, one can always shoot oneself with a gun (don't get me started on what I regard as the insane ubiquity of guns in the U.S.), hang oneself, jump off a cliff, crash a car at high speed into a bridge abutment, drown oneself, or employ some other means of obtaining death. But these are neither peaceful nor certain nor relatively dignified methods.

Trying to obtain lethal medications on the Internet from foreign countries is risky at best. There is no Food and Drug Administration beyond our borders, so you do not really know the composition of such a drug, nor do you know the shelf-life or how long it has already been sitting there.

## Consulting with a Doctor

William James Mayo, one of the founders of the Mayo Clinic, said: "The aim of medicine is to prevent disease and prolong life; the ideal of medicine is to eliminate the need of a physician." Most often one or more doctors are involved in our deaths. Yet I have maintained for decades that often we can eliminate the need of a physician. You do not need a doctor to die!

In medicine, the doctrine (or principle) of double effect is often invoked to explain the permissibility of an action that causes a serious harm, such as the death of a human being, as a side effect of promoting some good end. An example would be a sufficiently sympathetic doctor prescribing enough painkiller for you to kill yourself, knowing that is your goal, but ostensibly giving you the prescription to alleviate pain. The doctor (or compassionate hospice worker) might say something like "Now be careful, don't take too many or it might be trouble." Hospice per se is opposed to the right to die, but some hospice staff are not. This practice is legal and ethical.

An important note of caution: If you decide to talk with your doctor about the right to die without already knowing where your doctor stands on the issue, I strongly recommend doing so hypothetically and in the third person, saying something like: "My friend Barbara is really suffering and she is considering ending her life to avoid needless suffering. What do you think of that?" If you approach the subject directly, you could be involuntarily committed to a psychiatric institution for up to three days for being "a clear and present danger to yourself or others." I know three women in Arizona to whom this has happened!

And, speaking of doctors, what is wrong with this proclamation ,which I recently saw in a television advertisement? "Only your surgeon can tell if this surgery is right for you." Nonsense! Surgeons want to do surgery. Only you can tell whether it is right for you. The doctor is not God, and there is no need for unwarranted obeisance.

This reminds me of an old joke: A prominent and prosperous bank president dies and goes to heaven, only to encounter a very long line waiting at the pearly gates. The bank president goes to the front of the line and explains to Saint Peter: "I was an important and very virtuous person on earth. I was president of the bank. I was honest and fair, very philanthropic, headed numerous community organizations, my wife served with several charities, and my family was much beloved in our community. May I not then move to the front of the line?" Saint Peter tells the bank president that here in heaven all are treated equally and he must wait his turn in line to enter. A few minutes later a fellow dressed in green surgical scrubs walks right past the long line and straight through the pearly gates. Well, the bank president who is waiting is incensed and goes to Saint Peter and says, "What's the big idea? You told me I had to wait in line. How come that doctor just got to go right in?" To which Saint Peter replies: "Oh, that was not a doctor, that was God. He just likes to play doctor sometimes."

Here is another: What is the difference between God and a surgeon? God knows he's not a surgeon.

Of course you might want to consult a doctor, get a second opinion, know where your family and friends stand regarding your wishes and seek their advice, but ultimately it is simply up to you: your preferences and wishes are what must finally be honored. And only you can decide what you want or do not want. One reason there is too much surgery and not enough discussion at the end of life is that the health system will pay a doctor a lot for doing a surgical procedure and very little for having a frank, sensitive, hard conversation about end-of-life choices. Of course, doctors have those conversations anyway, every single day. But a side effect of the economics is that doctors do not have much incentive to learn about how to have those conversations. There is, however, good economic reason to go to conventions in beach resorts where you learn about new drugs, new devices and new surgeries, all underwritten by major corporations.

Most of us have worked hard to be able to control as much as we can regarding what happens in our lives. Why not exercise that control for the end of life?

> What's in a name? That which we call a rose by any other name would smell as sweet. So Romeo would, were he not Romeo call'd, retain that dear perfection which he owes without that title.
>
> — *Romeo and Juliet, Act II, Scene II*

## Don't Call it Suicide

There are many words and phrases used to describe the process of ending life:

- Autogenous Death
- Automortem
- Cathartic Death
- Consensual Murder
- Death With Dignity
- Deliberate Life Completion (My favorite shibboleth)
- Exiting
- Fulfilled Mortality
- Hastened Death
- Life-ending Choice
- Natural Death
- Non-adscititious Death
- Peaceful Death
- Prophylactic Suicide
- Rational end-of-life choice
- Self-Deliverance
- Self-Imposed Death
- Suicide
- Volitional Death
- Voluntary Death
- Medicide
- Terminal Sedation
- Patient-directed Dying
- Humane Self-chosen Death
- Choice in Dying
- Self-determined Death
- Aid in Dying
- Assisted Suicide
- Final Exit
- Managed Death
- Self-destruction
- Self-murder
- Self-directed death
- Peaceful Pill
- Drion Pill
- Stopping Eating and Drinking

I believe it is a mistake and an injustice to use the term "suicide," which has a pejorative connotation with significant stigma attached to it. After all, suicide ends a worthwhile life and ends all possibility of a worthwhile life.

A deeply ill person who requests a hastened death does not have that possibility. Suicide is frequently a hasty decision made during some immediate personal turmoil, and it is typically not peaceful, clean, or dignified, but rather messy, violent, and with an uncertain outcome.

By the way, the persistent myth that those who talk about it do not commit suicide is misleading. When one talks about killing oneself or not wanting to live any longer, it can be a serious warning sign that the person may well intend to act on such thoughts. Intervention is warranted.

It's worth noticing that one "commits suicide" and we usually associate the word "commit" with illegal activity, such as "committing a crime." In fact, suicide is not against the law in any state.

Envision a woman or man in the armed services fighting over in Iraq or Afghanistan. In an attempt to save his buddies, the soldier falls on an explosive sure to take his life. Do we call that action a "suicide," which Webster defines suicide as killing oneself because one no longer wishes to live? No. We more often than not look upon such acts as ones of heroism, and, many times, reward that person posthumously with some sort of hero's medal.

Shakespeare pondered this issue in *Henry V, Act IV*:

> But if the cause be not good, the king himself hath a heavy reckoning to make, when all those legs and arms and heads, chopped off in battle, shall join together at the latter day and cry all "We died at such a place;" some swearing, some crying for a surgeon, some upon their wives left poor behind them, some upon the debts they owe, some upon their children rawly left. I am afeard there are few die well that die in a battle; for how can they charitably dispose of anything, when blood is their argument? Now, if these men do not die well, it will be a black matter for the king that led them to it; whom to disobey were against all proportion of subjection.

Hundreds of people jumped to their deaths from the World Trade Center towers on September 11, 2001, to avoid the ravages of fire and destruction that occurred that terrible day. They chose a horrible death to avoid an even more horrible one. Nobody ever called those actions suicide. In fact, the coroner of New York officially characterized these deaths as homicides because third parties caused them.

To distinguish between suicide and a compassionately chosen hastened death, one might ask the following questions:

1. Is the chosen death harmful or helpful?
2. Is the chosen death irrational or rational?
3. Is the chosen death capricious or well-planned?
4. Is the chosen death regrettable or admirable?

If it is helpful, rational, well-planned, and admirable, then it is not suicide.

It can be a very rational choice to say, "I don't want to stick around through the bitter end, I am going to die anyway. I want to choose a peaceful death instead of an agonizing one."

Most of us do not want to die. We want, rather, to hang on as long as we can, as long as we can tolerate our suffering. But sometimes suffering gets so bad that all you want to do is go to sleep. When somebody is dying, and simply chooses to avoid those final agonizing stages, I don't see a tragedy, I see a blessing.

## Please Don't Impose Your Beliefs on Other People

One point I have made elsewhere needs to be repeated here.

If, because of your religious beliefs or other convictions, you would choose to suffer a long and painful death, I would support your right to make that choice. Only you can know how you prefer to die. The right-to-die movement is about personal choice. We respect other people's choices, and ask them not to impose their personal beliefs on those of us who wish to to have the right to choose self-deliverance.

## Treat Me Like a Dog

When I had to put my last golden retriever out of his misery, his death was peaceful and virtually instant. The veterinarian administered terminal sedation and Kingdom died with my arms around him, with no pain: not so much as a whimper. It was very sad but it was an act of kindness and he was gone the way most of us might prefer!

Isaac Asimov, referring to the book *Final Exit*, put it this way:

> No decent human being would allow an animal to suffer without putting it out of its misery. It is only to human beings that human beings are so cruel as to allow them to live on in pain, in hopelessness, in living death, without moving a muscle to help them. It is against such attitudes that this book fights.

A friend of mine called his longtime veterinarian to ask about hastening death. The veterinarian confided that he used to worry about the morality of euthanizing animals, and so he asked his Episcopal priest, "Is God okay with me taking life this way?" The priest told him that he was responsible for protecting life and that also meant protecting life from suffering. That, and 30 years of fervent thank-you notes from his patients' families, eased his mind. And then the veterinarian watched his mother's slow and painful death, and all he kept thinking was, "I would never let one of my patients suffer like this."

I sometimes wear a large circular button that proclaims in bright red letters on a yellow background: "Let me die like a dog!" Do you think that Fido or Fluffy would ask for your help to die, if they could? And how much more important is it to allow that mercy to a human being who wants and requests help in dying?

## The Very Best Ways to Hasten One's Own Death

If it were done, then t'were well it were done quickly.

— *Hamlet*

If one is intent on hastening one's death, the two best means that I know of to obtain a certain, peaceful, and painless end of life are the helium method and voluntary stopping of eating and drinking (VSEAD, sometimes called VSED). These can bring about certain death with dignity or — to use my preferred phrase once more — deliberate life completion. The helium method takes about ten to fifteen minutes, and VSEAD takes on average about fifteen days or maybe as short a time as one week.

With VSEAD, after all oral intake stops, there usually is a period that lasts for at least several days and sometimes longer before the patient becomes completely unconscious, depending on the patient's pre-fasting condition. This interval provides an opportunity for the patient to reflect and reconsider the VSEAD decision, and for family members to come to understand and accept that the desire to hasten death truly is what the patient wants.

It is, in fact, quite possible to will oneself to die. Elderly people sometimes subtly do this. It's called "turning your face to the wall." If you stop eating, interacting with people, or taking care of yourself, you will eventually get sick and die. And people who stop drinking liquids will die even sooner. People with severe drug addictions sometimes do it unintentionally by being unconscious too much of the time and not hydrating between highs.

It seems counterintuitive, but with the VSAED method one is not always hungry. The human body quickly adapts itself to the situation as one's organs slowly begin to shut down. This is almost always without pain, and securing a peaceful death this way on average takes fifteen days. It may be quicker, or may be slightly longer. One can readily find a wealth of information about VSEAD on the Internet.

While surfing the Internet, you might stumble across sources of lethal medications from other countries. As noted earlier in this chapter, this is risky at best, as you do not really know the composition of the drugs, nor do you know the shelf-life or how long it has already been sitting there.

## The Helium Method

You can learn how to use the helium method from Derek Humphry's book or the DVD *Final Exit*, which is probably in your local library or local bookstore, or you may order a copy from The Euthanasia Research & Guidance Organization (ERGO) at *http://www.finalexit.org/ergo-store*. ERGO also sells instructions about how best to make the necessary hood, which contains the gas.

I highly recommend, if using the helium method, that you have an exit guide with you to make sure that you do it properly. Such a guide is available free to members of Final Exit Network (*www.finalexitnetwork.org*) after some initial evaluation and screening.

The helium method (also possible with other types of inert gas), is my own choice as the best method to obtain a quick, certain and peaceful death, but needless to say, it should be carefully considered.

How long does it take? While there is no definitive answer, it is safe to say that one will be rendered unconscious within a few minutes and will be dead within ten to fifteen minutes. I have been with half a dozen people who used this method and all went well. I have a friend who has been with over two hundred people who died this way and, again, all went well. It is best to leave the hood on longer, perhaps an hour or more. There is no danger in leaving the helium on until the tanks are emptied.

Among those I have accompanied who used this method, it was never an easy decision for them. While not fearful of the actual death process, they were saddened about leaving this world: all they had known, all that they loved, all that they treasured. Their grief was enormous. All had put their affairs in order, but one of them still worried about squabbles over the estate's assets.

## Avoiding Legal Liability

Some people choose to use the helium method covertly, having someone else remove the equipment after the death, while others do so overtly, maybe with a note explaining their reasons for choosing to die, clearly stating that no one else helped, and/or a copy of *Final Exit* at their side. It is entirely up to the individual. In any case, when an unexpected death occurs at home, the police are usually summoned, so be sure no one else's fingerprints are on any of the equipment used.

In some cases I know about, the supporting individual (not an Exit Guide, but a friend or family member) left the one who wanted to die on their own for several hours to accomplish the task. During that time the support person drove out of town, making sure to use his credit card at a distant location to show he was not present at the time of death (although there is nothing illegal about being with someone at the time of death). Upon returning, the body was discovered and then the death reported.

One way to lessen the chance of unwanted inquiry by the authorities is to be enrolled in hospice care at the time of death. Then a friend or family member just calls the hospice when you have died. "Failure to thrive" can be a criterion for hospice admission, and each hospice has its own requirements for this, such as having lost twenty percent of body weight within three months, etc. Again, a sympathetic physician can be of great help in getting one admitted to hospice care. Note that the national hospice organization is opposed to self-inflicted hastened death, so do not let them know what you are planning. Yet there are many understanding hospice workers who may well support your wish to die this way.

It should also be noted that even without hospice involvement, a patient who is near life's end, under regular care of a doctor, can usually die at home without police involvement. Needless to say, the doctor must be called to issue a death certificate.

## Answers to Other Common Questions

For maximum efficiency, it helps to take a deep breath and then strongly exhale before pulling the bag or hood down over your head. It also helps to gently compress or squeeze the hood to the contours of your head after you exhale in order to remove excess air.

One does not crap their pants automatically at the time of death when using this method, so there is no need to wear a diaper, though one may want to relieve oneself beforehand in any case. The sudden loss of bowel control usually occurs only with violent methods such as hanging.

There is no feeling of suffocation or "oxygen hunger." One is simply comfortably breathing the inert gas instead of oxygen.

The shelf life of the helium tanks is about two years. One can check by simply turning on the valve about one-eighth of the way to hear the hissing sound of gas being emitted, or purchase a regulator with a gauge indicating how much gas is remaining.

Having a pacemaker or implanted defibrillator is not a problem.

Since helium is lighter than air, it is important not to be lying down, as that could cause some of the gas to escape. One must be sitting up in a secure position, perhaps propped up on both sides with pillows or cushions.

## Be Sure the Helium is Not Diluted

There is no magic about helium compared to other inert gases such as nitrogen. Helium used to be easily obtained in party balloon kits, but many of those are now diluted with twenty percent air, and will not serve this purpose. One could use a different gas, but full-strength helium is still available from a number of sources.

As this goes to press, FEN is doing some trials with nitrogen, in case helium does become less available. The diluted version will not work, so you need to be sure. In the meantime, if using the balloon kit, be sure to check the labeling on the box or ask the store if it is pure helium. Some I have seen recently said "Helium, Air" and others said "Helium, Compressed." Do not use the one with air.

There are at least two major suppliers of inert gas with multiple retail outlets throughout the country. Their tanks come in several sizes, and they foresee no shortfall of helium (contrary to some recent rumors that the gas is becoming scarce). They carry balloon adapters, and sell largely to industries but will also sell to the general public. A tank containing 30 or 60 cubic feet of compressed helium is more than sufficient. And with their stronger steel tanks, the helium will probably last longer than it did in some of the older tanks sold at regular retail outlets. Keep in mind, however, that no store personnel will advise you on use.

## DO NOT ANNOUNCE YOUR PURPOSE

Of course, you must not announce your intent. Say the helium is to inflate balloons for a huge party you're having or some other purpose. There are a number of other uses of helium: for observation in quantum mechanics; as lightweight aircraft fuel; for use by caisson workers; use by divers with oxygen during their dives; or to cool down superconduction magnets. Welding companies also rely on it to provide protection. It is used the same way in the development of titanium, zirconium, germanium and silicon. Helium also has medical applications: it may be used for breathing observation. It is essential in treating ailments such as asthma, emphysema, and other conditions that affect breathing. The gas is usually used to treat diseases that affect the lungs.

An affiliate of Final Exit Network conducts comprehensive demonstrations of the helium method about four times a year for FEN members only. I would estimate that over 150 people have participated in such demonstrations here in the Tucson area, wherein they receive much more information than I have given above, including numerous handouts, a video illustration, and an opportunity to manipulate the equipment themselves.

## BUT REMEMBER, HELIUM IS JUST ONE OPTION

The choice to end one's life with helium is still controversial in America and much of the rest of the world. I worry that some people might open this book solely to find that information. While I believe that a person who is suffering greatly with no chance of relief should have a right to choose their time of death in the least painful way, some of the other options have greater acceptance by leaders of medical organizations and many major religions.

These are all covered in this book, but are worthy of a brief summary here to maintain perspective:

- Respecting living wills and powers of attorney in health matters, by not performing CPR or other lifesaving procedures;
- Patient refusal of interventions or treatment;
- Removal of life-sustaining interventions, such as endotracheal tubes and gastric feeding tubes, with medication as needed for comfort;
- Patient refusal of nutrition and hydration;
- Doctor increasing pain medication to the point that it hastens, though is not intended to cause, death: the "Double Effect";
- "Terminal Sedation," in which the patient is anesthetized to a comatose state until death occurs by starvation and dehydration.

For emphasis, I need to repeat that in no way am I talking about mercy killing or taking the life of someone else. This is strictly about a competent adult ending his or her own life! There is a world of difference between killing someone and allowing someone to die. While many states use a DNR form (Do Not Resuscitate) some are changing the DNR to a phrase I much prefer: AND (Allow Natural Death).

You might do well to ask yourself how you envision your aging process. What are your concerns? What do you want for yourself? What causes you the most discomfort?

Of course physician aid in dying is legal in several states, including Washington, Oregon, Vermont, California, and Colorado. Although legal, it is not always easy, and it is expensive — obtaining the lethal prescription can cost $3,000 to $4,000. And even in Oregon, where this has been legal for nineteen years, it is difficult to find a doctor who will comply. And in California whole hospital chains and many doctors have refused to participate. There are well-established criteria and procedures and, perhaps more importantly, there have been no instances of abuse of such laws. Many of those who obtain a lethal prescription do not end up using it. They, and many others, are greatly comforted by the knowledge that death is an option and is available if they need it.

As it stands now, one out of every six Americans has access to a physician's aid in dying. As the right-to-die movement strengthens, more and more people will gain such access. As I have stated previously, physician aid in dying is still not comprehensive enough, but it is a big step forward. In recent decades, substantial progress (though of course not enough) has been made in women's rights, LGBT rights, the rights of racial and religious minorities, and rights of the disabled. We are now entering an era of slow advancements in the right to choose a dignified death.

# How to Navigate a Medical Environment 12

Illness and death can arrive unexpectedly and find us unprepared. This chapter details some specific advice for entering a medical environment.

Most Americans report that they would prefer to die at home, with treatment to keep them comfortable. But a report from the Institute of Medicine found that the reality for most people often includes unwanted invasive care and not enough comfort, in part because too few people make their wishes known in advance to their doctors, friends, and families.

The word "treat" comes from the Latin root *tractare,* which means "to drag, draw or pull." And the Latin *patiens* means "one who suffers." So when a doctor treats a patient, it historically means that person "passively suffers." That sure does not sound good to me.

In no way do I mean to disparage doctors, but frankly the facts are scary. According to the November 2014 issue of *Consumer Reports*, hospital errors are the third leading cause of death in the United States, and up to thirty percent of patients suffer serious problems after surgery, including infections, heart attacks, strokes, or other complications.

A 2010 study from the U.S. Department of Health and Human Services estimated that 180,000 Medicare beneficiaries alone die every year from medical accidents and errors. About 400,000 drug-related injuries occur every year in hospitals, according to an Institute of Medicine study. Five to ten percent of patients get a preventable infection in the hospital, and nearly 100,000 people die from one each year, reported the Centers for Disease Control and Prevention. Nobody has exact numbers, and many of these are not reported. But in 2016, it was estimated that errors and preventable infections killed about 800,000 patients in total. That is the equivalent of six jumbo jets crashing every day!

I think that American hospitals today really do not provide much in the way of end-of-life care. They seem to provide bodily repair services under the direction of independent physicians, scientists, and nurses on a schedule that is not yours. Death is timed in hospitals: know how to advocate there, or avoid being there. The best way to manage a terminal hospitalization is not to have one. With that said, I will offer some rules of thumb that could help in the case of a hospitalization.

## Bring an Advocate, Especially for Check-in and Discharge

Even for relatively routine hospital visits, another set of eyes and ears monitoring your care helps. It is difficult, at best, to be your own advocate when hospitalized. Surely you are feeling pretty puny in the first place or you would not be in the hospital. You may be confronted with a morass of information, and you're wearing one of those dehumanizing hospital gowns that leaves your buttocks flapping in the wind, and constantly getting poked and probed by various medical personnel.

## Sanitize, Sanitize, Sanitize

Guard against super-bugs by using alcohol and bleach wipes on surfaces. Bring a big bottle of hand sanitizer, put it by your bed, and remind everyone to keep hands clean. You (or your advocate) may feel awkward asking everyone who enters your room to properly wash their hands. Do it anyway. Every year, nearly two million infections are spread in hospitals. The Centers for Disease Control and Prevention (CDC) estimates that this number could be reduced by as much as seventy percent if health-care workers would consistently wash their hands before and after treating each patient.

Do not let anyone in the hospital touch you until:

- You have seen him/her wash hands, either in a sink or with an alcohol-based gel sanitizer. You can say something like, "I'm sorry, but I'm really afraid of infections. Would you mind washing your hands before we start?"
- You have seen him wash before he puts on gloves. The gloves won't protect you if they are contaminated from unwashed hands.
- The person has wiped and sanitized instruments that will touch you, including blood pressure cuffs and stethoscopes.

## Be Vigilant and Ask Questions

- When in a hospital, it is important to ask for a daily list of medications and doses, and check them.
- If you have tubes in you, have them traced back to the source. (Sometimes you may end up connected to either the wrong dosage or the wrong substance altogether.)

- Bring a notebook. Write down all your medications, why you take them, and who prescribed them. Include phone numbers of key medical contacts.
- When questions arise in the hospital, write them down.
- Take your cell phone and charger.
- Check credentials. Make sure the hospital is accredited by the Joint Commission, which is the chief hospital accreditation organization in the U.S. (*www.qualitycheck.org*).
- "Overwhelming data show that when patients actively participate in their own care, they have better outcomes," says Peter J. Pronovost, MD, patient safety expert at Johns Hopkins. Be watchful and persistent. Make sure providers follow standard procedures for common practices such as inserting IV lines.

Dr. David Shulkin of Beth Israel Medical Center has described the consequences when patients are too trustful or too reserved:

> As the chief executive of a major medical center, I have reviewed dozens of cases in which patients knew something was wrong with their care but were too polite, too uncomfortable or too intimidated to speak up.
>
> Example: One woman didn't say anything when she was called by the wrong name. She just went along — and wound up having extensive tests that were intended for another patient.
>
> No serious harm was done in this case, but others aren't so lucky. I've seen people needlessly suffer severe pain because they didn't want to question their doctor's judgment...or risk a serious infection because they felt that it was rude to tell someone to wash his/her hands.
>
> It's normal to feel intimidated in the authoritarian environment of a doctor's office or a medical center — but it's better to be tough. Studies show that so-called difficult patients, ones who demand the highest level of care, recover more quickly and with fewer complications than those who are passive.

## Stopping a Procedure

You are never required to continue a treatment or procedure that is going badly. For example, a nurse might fail to properly insert an intravenous (IV) needle after multiple attempts, or a resident might have a hard time doing a spinal tap.

When someone has a needle in your back, it might not feel like the best time to complain, but it is your right to do so: to ask someone else to take over, or even to stop the procedure.

At teaching hospitals, many procedures are done by residents. If a procedure or treatment is taking too long or causing too much pain, ask for a more experienced attending physician to take over. You could say something like, "This seems to be taking too long. I would appreciate having someone with more experience try." If the staff argues — or, worse, ignores you — ask to speak to a nursing supervisor.

Ask a friend or family member to be present during procedures. Patients understandably are reluctant to challenge their health-care team. An advocate, however, is more dispassionate and can watch out for your best interests. He/she might say something like, "1 think she has had enough. We need to take a break for a moment."

Be prepared to learn what "no" sounds like, emerging from your or your proxy's mouth, even in response to a routine procedure like a blood test, which may be painful to you and could be phony posturing, as if the staff is professing to look for "cures" though you are terminal.

"It's almost impossible for patients really to be in charge," says Joanne Lynn, a physician and the director of the nonprofit Altarum Center for Elder Care and Advanced Illness in Washington, D.C. "We enforce a kind of learned helplessness, especially in hospitals." I asked her how much unwanted treatment gets administered. She couldn't come up with a figure — no one can — but she said, "It's huge, however you measure it. Especially when people get very, very sick."

## Asking for More Drugs

It is common for patients to needlessly suffer post-surgical pain because they do not want to seem like complainers or because they are afraid that their doctors will suspect they are drug abusers, but adequate pain control is critical. Patients who experience little or no pain are more ambulatory, less likely to get pneumonia, have a lower risk for blood clots and leave the hospital, on average, one to two days sooner than those whose pain is managed poorly.

Many physicians and nurses now routinely ask patients if they feel any pain and, if so, to rate it on a scale of one to ten. There are no tests that can accurately gauge a patient's pain, so these self-reports are critical, and it is important to do this even if you are not asked. Opioid epidemics are now reaching crisis proportions in some parts of the country, prompting increased caution in prescribing them, but addiction is rare when drugs are used for temporary pain relief — and doctors know this.

Never assume that your level of pain is normal. If you think the pain is intolerable, it needs to be treated. Make sure that your pain is taken seriously. Sometimes asking a patient to rate pain one to ten is so much of a routine that the nurse or doctor pays no attention to your answer, so you may need to request a pain assessment.

In a formal pain assessment, you will probably be asked the one-to-ten scale question again. Most patients can be brought down to levels of two or below with the right medication. If you need a higher dose, or more frequent dosing, say so. Your doctor will understand if you say that the pain treatment is not working. Everyone responds to painkillers differently.

## Doorway Visits

A hospital doctor will sometimes poke his or her head in your doorway, ask how you are doing, and then rush off before you have a chance to discuss concerns.

If you are nervous about confronting the doctor directly, or the doctor never sticks around long enough for you to say anything, keep a notebook by your bedside. Write down your questions and concerns. Then, when the doctor is present, hold up the notebook and say something like, "I am glad you're here. I have just a few issues that I have written down. I would like to go through them with you."

## Negotiating Fees

Do not be embarrassed to discuss financial issues with your doctor's office or the hospital, particularly if you do not have insurance. Negotiating fees and payment schedules is routine.

For example, suppose that you have recently lost your job and health insurance. Bring it up the next time you see your doctor. Say something like, "I want to make sure that I get the best care, but I don't have health insurance right now. Cost is important, so I would be grateful if we could discuss it."

Doctors often reduce fees for patients who do not have insurance. They also can reduce costs in other ways, such as prescribing generic rather than brand-name drugs, ordering only essential tests, and scheduling telephone follow-ups rather than office visits.

> "Don't worry," he would say, smiling. "Dying is much more difficult than one imagines."
>
> — Gabriel García Márquez, *One Hundred Years of Solitude*

# Practical Steps When Preparing for Death 13

This chapter offers details that may be helpful when navigating the inevitable tasks that will need to be done before and after someone dies. It may serve you well to give these tasks some forethought.

Another good tool is the booklet titled *Before I Go You Should Know,* made available by the Funeral Consumers Alliance (*www.funerals.org*). A "Death Check List" is not very warm or fuzzy, but it contains many pragmatic considerations.

This listing should be useful regardless of whether you are preparing for your own death or assisting in planning for a family member. Some items may not apply to your circumstance, but because every situation is different, I try to include as many potential issues as possible.

In many cases, most of the steps below are carried out by a funeral director or a lawyer, and some people may have assistance from a church group, memorial society, or organization such as Funeral Consumers Alliance.

And of course, families that handle funeral arrangements themselves (rather than paying a funeral director) have extra responsibilities such as preparing the body, possibly making arrangements for organ or whole body donation, getting transit permits, transporting the body to a gravesite or crematory, burial permits, registering with the municipal clerk if burial is on private property, obtaining death certificates, and more. Green burial and home burial are becoming increasingly popular, which I applaud because when loved ones have an intimate "hands on" role, it usually helps with the bereavement process.

## When Death is Approaching

- Investigate the possibilities of hospice care or other care.
- Complete or update the Point of Contact list of who is to be notified.
- Choose your advocate (see Chapter 9) and inform that person of your wishes surrounding end-of-life care.

- Locate and update your will (remembering that 401Ks and life insurance policies are not governed by a will).
- Update and distribute copies of all advance directives (see Chapter 9 for list of documents).
- Make decisions and inform physician of desires concerning organ/tissue donation. If so, where is the permission card, what part(s) of body are to go where?
- Remember, Power of Attorney ends at death, so specify who will control the body. Legally, in most cases, this will be your "next of kin" or somebody designated with approval of your next of kin.
- If need be, make arrangements for the care of pets.
- Make arrangements for elimination or preservation of your digital data. Yes, you can scratch out your existence from cyberspace. (The companies that keep our data in cyberspace have confusing, inconsistent, or non-existent policies about this.) You can use a "digital estate" service, thus naming a digital executor along with a regular executor in your will. There are services available to manage your digital data: *https://www.backupify.com/about-us* (to preserve your digital existence) or *http://www.suicidemachine.org* (to eradicate your digital existence).

## Write Down, in One Place, Your Funeral Plans

- Name, address, phone of person with legal right to handle funeral arrangements.
- Name, address and phone of funeral director you desire (if any).
- If you have a cemetery plot, give location, plot number, and plot location.
- What kind of grave marker do you wish?
- Do you wish to be cremated? If so, indicate what to do with the cremains.
- Make instructions concerning selection of coffin and vault.
- Do you wish to have a viewing (calling hours) at the funeral home?
- List anything special (clothing, jewelry, etc.) you wish to be included in your burial or cremation coffin.
- If you wish a memorial service, is it to be public or private?
- Name, address and phone of any clergy who should be notified.
- Special requests for the service (hymns, readings, participants, etc.)
- Do you wish flowers to be sent or donations made in memory? To whom and where?

- Name, address and phone of people you would like to have as pallbearers.

## WRITE DOWN, IN ONE PLACE, ALL LEGAL/FINANCIAL PLANS

- Location of will.
- Name of executor.
- Location of any trusts, deeds, living will, power of attorney, etc.
- Location of safety deposit box and key — empty the box if need be.
- Name, address and phone of your attorney.
- Listing of all checking and savings accounts, with numbers and location of documents.
- Listing and location of insurance policies and numbers, pension plans, etc.
- Location of birth certificate, marriage license/certificate, divorce papers, adoption papers, discharge papers, corporate papers.
- Location of medical records, prescriptions, etc.
- Location of tax returns for the past 3–5 years.
- Location of Social Security card(s).
- Location of car titles, mortgage, purchase agreements, other property papers.
- Credit cards and charge accounts to be canceled.
- Statement of burial costs to whom?
- And add additional information you would like family or friends to know (such as who gets diamond ring, antique clock, etc., if not already specified in your will).

## STEPS FOR NEXT OF KIN AFTER A DEATH

- Make a decision concerning a discretionary autopsy, if you believe there may be a reason for one.
- Contact those responsible to complete donation of organs (this is time sensitive).
- Locate will and review for instructions related to funeral.
- Locate other burial instructions, if any.
- Determine which funeral home will be used, if any.
- Contact funeral director, crematory, memorial society, or medical school.
- Determine date and time for visitation, if any.

- Determine date and time for memorial service and/or burial, considering availability of family and friends to attend, church, funeral home, and cemetery.
- Determine if photos of deceased or other objects are desired for the service or reception. If so, collect or scan for a slide show.
- Ask someone to stay in the home during funeral and request police drive-by if that seems appropriate. Burglars strike when they know you are away.
- Consider special needs of the household, such as cleaning, etc., done by friends.
- Determine whether a post-funeral reception is desired, and make arrangements.
- Determine vehicle and driver requirements: home to and from church, and to and from cemetery.
- Determine which guests need transportation to or from airport.
- Select and contact minister/clergy and/or other person(s) giving eulogy.
- Contact organist, soloist, or other musicians.
- Contact pallbearers.
- Order flowers, if desired.
- Arrange for payment of honoraria to musicians, minister, etc.
- Choose clothes for the deceased.
- Contact friends, relatives, executor of the will, and business associates.
- Choose cemetery plot, columbarium, or other appropriate means for final disposition, if that has not already been arranged prior to death.
- Arrange for someone to answer phone and door, keeping careful records of calls.
- Arrange hospitality for visiting relatives and friends.
- Determine if guest book attendants are needed.
- Purchase clothing for yourself, if necessary.
- Make appointment with hairstylist, if necessary. Make arrangements for child care, if necessary.

## Writing an Obituary

The following are suggestions to consider, keeping in mind that most newspapers now charge by the number of words or lines. Obviously, not all of these items are applicable in all cases.

- Full legal name, and maiden name if different.
- Legal residence and years at address.
- Date and place of birth.
- Preceded in death by ...
- Survived by: spouse, parents, children, siblings, significant friends and relatives.
- If married, give full name of spouse, date and place of marriage.
- If widowed, give full name of spouse and date and place of death.
- If divorced and former spouse is still living, give name and place of residence.
- Name and birthplace of father, current residence if living.
- Name and birthplace of mother, current residence if living.
- Names of other significant friends and relatives.
- If the deceased is a veteran, date and place of enlistment, date and place of discharge, rank or rating, service number, organization or outfit, commendations received.
- Educational background.
- Occupation and past position of employment.
- Religious affiliation.
- Membership in churches, clubs, and organizations.
- Any major awards received.
- If flowers are omitted, and donations requested for a cause, include it in obituary.
- Most obituaries fail to cite the cause of death. I wish they did so, and hope you will consider including that information.

## Steps for Survivors to Take After the Funeral

- Plan for the disposition of flowers.
- Prepare a list of distant persons who need to be notified by letter or printed notice.
- Order copies of the death certificate through the funeral director or county or municipal recorder's office. Sometimes as many as 20 may be needed.
- Begin applying for any appropriate survivor benefits.
- Contact life insurance company for claim forms, for yourself or others who may be beneficiaries. Request only the funds you need to live on until you can consult with a financial adviser.

- See an attorney who can explain the terms of the will, and file the will with courts, if these arrangements have not already been made by the deceased.
- Begin probate proceedings, if necessary.
- Petition the court for appointment as executor if that has not been specified by the deceased in his/her will.
- Locate important documents.
- Check Social Security office for any benefits that may be due for eligible survivors.
- If the deceased is a veteran, contact the Veterans Administration for possible survivor benefits: *www.va.gov.*
- Begin applying for any appropriate survivor benefits.
- Send medical claims to the appropriate insurance carriers.
- Consult with a financial adviser about how to request large-sum benefits.
- Contact credit card and charge card companies.
- Change billing name with utility companies.
- Change registration on vehicles by contacting Department of Motor Vehicles.
- Contact rental and lease companies.
- Cancel health club and other memberships, as well as subscriptions.

## Additional Steps if You are the Executor

- Open a bank account to facilitate money due the estate.
- Inventory all assets.
- Collect all monies due the estate.
- Apply for a tax identification number.
- File Form 56, Notice Concerning Fiduciary Relationship.
- Send thank you notes and acknowledgments.
- See an accountant for a tax projection.
- Review all insurance with your agent to see if coverage is appropriate and adequate.
- Change beneficiaries if needed on insurance policies, retirement accounts, saving bonds, etc.
- Transfer all assets into your name or into trust accounts, following directions in the will.
- Make a plan for paying debts and obligations. Some may carry insurance clauses that will cancel them. If there is to be a delay in

meeting payments, consult with creditors and ask for more time before the payments are due.

- Make necessary decisions concerning deceased's self-employment business, if relevant.
- List claims against estate.
- Liquidate assets as necessary to pay bills.
- Prepare tax returns and pay tax liabilities.
- Pay all bills.
- Disburse assets to heirs.
- Prepare an accounting for the courts.
- Advise beneficiaries of new tax basis for assets.
- Close probate.

## STEPS FOR SURVIVORS WHO MUST ADJUST TO LIFE CHANGES

In some cases I have encountered surviving spouses who have never driven a car, written a check, or gained experience with other practical matters. Those are relatively rare cases, but any survivor who is affected financially by the death will need to take a number of actions. Here is a sample list. Note that some of them should not be rushed unnecessarily during the emotional period of initial grief.

- Update your will.
- Prepare a net-worth statement.
- Make a list of income and expenses.
- Track your expenses to see where your money is being spent.
- Seek professional counseling or grief workshop.
- Go through old records and files, including canceled checks for clues to any additional benefits, assets, or obligations.
- Choose a memorial marker.
- Create a new budget.
- Apply for credit in your own name.
- Begin gathering information for tax returns.
- Explore alternatives for future living arrangements.
- Make plans for your future (life and career).
- Begin to think about investments.
- Investigate support groups and clubs.

# A Few Words on Grief

# 14

*She could forgive him for missing their dinner date,*
*but she would never forgive him for dying.*
— Chrys Fey, *30 Seconds*

GRIEF, MOURNING, AND BEREAVEMENT ARE not the focus of this book, but the emotional issues are still part of the experience of dying: for the one dying who is about to lose everything and everyone, and for the survivors losing a loved one. We have all experienced grief, and have developed certain feelings and attitudes toward being confronted with death.

Sometimes tension is exacerbated by material concerns. My friend "Timothy" (not his real name) had been a classmate, had done parish field work with me, and was a fellow motorcycle rider. When his mother died, he and his sister were at one of the family estates to make arrangements for distribution of assets. Timothy was already independently wealthy with a net worth of about 12 million dollars as, presumably, was his sister. Yet during their stay together, Timothy had his private room independently alarmed, fearful that his sister might kill him in order to inherit more money. I was quite taken aback by this, and saddened. Such a thought would never occur to me. Perhaps Timothy had dwelt too much on the biblical Matthew 10:36: "...and a man's enemies will be the members of his household."

Grief is almost universal, even when a death has been anticipated. I have found that one is never really ready for death. Although I have been working in this field for decades, it is a most profound and unsettling experience when a person I love is permanently gone.

Death may be an ineffable experience that is simply and profoundly beyond words. When you try to describe it in words, you just cannot do it. My father died eight years ago to the month as I write this, yet not a day goes by that I do not think of him: his typically British sense of humor, his brilliance. He was an avid reader and probably the smartest person I have ever met. Even in his nineties he was still practicing his Spanish. He had a kind, soft-spoken, no-nonsense demeanor, and a tendency to understate things. For example, if he said "Joe is alright," that could mean that Joe hung the moon. To this day I am not very good at giving compliments, though I am working on it.

There is no way to avoid having someone you love die, and there are only two ways you can avoid grief and bereavement: you can live without giving a damn, not caring, or you can die as an infant. That's it. And I hope that when your someone dies, it is not badly.

My friend, hero, and fellow thanatologist, Rabbi Earl Grollman, has collected statements straight from the mouths of those who had lost a loved one. He writes:

> Grief is a process, not an event. Listen to the words of the teachers — the bereaved who share their thoughts with us as to when they know that the sun is finally peeping through the clouds:
>
> - I can find something to laugh about.
> - I like going to the cemetery but I don't have to go as often.
> - I disposed of some memory marks without feeling disloyal.
> - I attend funerals and am able to focus on that person who died rather than my own loss.
> - I go to the support group mostly to help the other bereaved people, no longer for myself.
> - I sleep better and am not so tired all the time.
> - I now like looking at the photographs.

Grief is the expression of mourning. The best one can do is reconcile oneself to the death by making the transition of having the deceased one go from a presence to a memory.

A risk associated with reflecting upon death is simply one's attitude toward it. Very recently the *Journal of Psychology & Aging* yielded research conducted by the National Institutes of Health's chief scientist on brain aging showing long-term effects of certain negative attitudes. If a person harbors negative stereotypes about aged people, believing they are less sharp, slower, and unhappier than younger people, then decades later, that person is more likely to exhibit the brain changes seen in Alzheimer's disease. Believing that older people are afflicted with cognitive, physical, financial, and sexual woes causes stress in those headed in the same direction: aging. This stress takes a toll.

And there is more research to back this up. Johns Hopkins and the National Institute on Aging, through the Baltimore Longitudinal Study on Aging, showed significant detrimental brain changes linked to Alzheimer's in those who harbored more negative attitudes than those who had a more positive outlook. A 2011 study published in "Proceedings of the National

Academy of Sciences" found that older people who reported being the least happy died at nearly twice the rate in the next five years as people who reported being the most happy. When we respect our elders, we reap benefits for ourselves!

It is Thanksgiving as I write this part. I am reminded of the words of William Bradford, who helped found the Plymouth Colony and served as Plymouth Colony Governor five times between 1621 and 1657.

For them a place did God provide
in wilderness and then guide
unto the American shore
where they make way for many more.
They broke the ice, themselves alone
and so became a stepping stone
for all others who in like case
were glad to find a resting place.

Just as some of the first American settlers provided guidance for those who came after them, so may those who are dying and those who grieve.

# Some Concluding Thoughts 15

Human suffering takes many forms, and it is important for us as advocates to consider the broad spectrum. We live in a "Have a nice day" society, not acknowledging suffering. Throughout much of my tenure as a parish priest, I longed for more reality in church in this regard. Churches frequently display signs and banners proclaiming "Joy" or "Love" or "Peace" or "Hope." These are all well and good, but I would like to see some banners recognizing other inevitable aspects of life, such as "Pain" or "Suffering" or even "God Dammit." (I believe God is big enough to take it.) Why can we not admit the existence of these?

Several European countries should be lauded for their dealing realistically with the desperation, helplessness, and hopelessness that so many people experience near life's end.

I believe that it is incumbent upon our society to allocate more resources to address the fact that 120 Americans kill themselves every day. Both psychological and physical distress must be addressed, with a clear recognition that physical illness and decline are among many factors that can make life seem no longer worth living.

The terminally ill tell us that suffering may take the shape of abandonment, anticipatory grief, anxiety, confusion, delirium, dependence on others, depression, fear, futility, hopelessness, loneliness, loss, psychic pain, tiredness of life, or unworthy dying

Regrettably, our society is reluctant to acknowledge or legitimatize suffering, let alone assign it any merit, nobility, or honor. Perhaps we as advocates can change that. We may assist and permit the dying to at least acknowledge and honor their own suffering , and we may teach others to do so as well.

Or perhaps we can minimize the suffering considerably. The press, the public, and politicians may not be convinced, but plenty of scientists believe that they can render us less sick at the end of our lives. By manipulating senescent cells, and by eliminating the sticky stuff found in the brains of deceased Alzheimer's patients, and by manipulating genes, and working with chemistry and medications, they are determined to modify the aging process to achieve longer and healthier lives for all of us.

There is much good research being done about Alzheimer's, which is not just the end stage, but a journey to the grave, a slow death by a thousand cuts. Chief risk factors include: family history, head injury, Alzheimer's marker genes, gender, age, and stroke/emotional trauma.

It seems that exercise, the equivalent of at least 10,000 steps a day, is a key to reducing risks. And one must also engage in social interaction, exercise the brain daily, and eat a healthful diet — a Mediterranean diet of fruits, vegetables, nuts, olive oil, less red meat, and Omega-3 fatty acids are advised. Sound sleep, at least seven hours a night, is essential, experts say, in shielding and retaining memory.

From what I have been reading lately, it seems that indeed exercise can not only reduce the risk of Alzheimer's disease but may well help us reduce the risk of everything from catching the flu to getting cancer. Apparently it can be quite salubrious. Says Stephanie Linderman from the American Federation for Aging Research: "Every scientist, no matter what they are working on, will always say, 'Try to exercise just a little bit more and eat as many plant-based foods as possible.'" And from Doctor Nir Barzilia, director of the Institute for Aging Research at the Albert Einstein College of Medicine: "Exercise is probably the most healthy thing you can do."

There are very promising trials underway with drugs that target the disease in various ways to either prevent or cure Alzheimer's Disease. Doctor Frank Longo, chairman of the department of neurology and neurological sciences at Stanford University says "My biggest frustration is that we have cured Alzheimer's in mice many times. Why can't we move that success to people?"

No one knows what the future holds, but this ravishing disease of forgetfulness may one day be vanquished by learning how to manipulate and modify memory. Scientists are now doing this in lab animals with the use of optogenetics. Specific memories can be implanted or edited.

On another level, imagine what this development of altering memories could mean for the mourning process and the expression of grief over someone's death. After all, mourning is the process by which people incorporate the experience of loss into their ongoing lives while in the state of being bereaved.

Scientists, physicians, and other researchers from the following, among others, have been working in the field of the science of aging to slow down the process of aging: University of Illinois at Chicago; Albert Einstein College of Medicine; American Federation for Aging Research; Novartis Institutes for Biomedical Research; Venture Capitalists for Biology; University of Alabama at Birmingham, Department of Biology; GE Global Research

Center; McGill University, Department of Medicine and Oncology; Buck Institute for Research on Aging; Mayo Clinic; University of Pennsylvania, Department of Medical Ethics and Health Policy; and University of California San Francisco, School of Medicine.

Another similar endeavor is undertaken by an organization working in the field of alternative medicine and a holistic approach to health: the Life Extension Foundation, a collection of physicians who sponsor clinical trials of food and natural supplements as a way to prevent/treat/cure disease and to extend our life spans, the only such research of its kind in the U.S.

As you can see, many are striving to keep the bloom on the rose longer and to kick the can down the road farther. We have already made significant advances through medicine and technology in increasing the human lifespan. Someone born in 1900 could expect to live to about age fifty. Someone born today may expect to live to reach about age eighty.

Thus far, researchers can change a single gene in a worm and have that worm live twice as long as is normal. Fruit flies have also been made to live longer. And slowing aging has been demonstrated in mice as well. All of this leads some to believe that it is plausible and possible to slow aging for humans. Now their goal is persuade the Food and Drug Administration that some test trials in humans are warranted. These researchers hope to show that slowing aging will influence fatal and disabling diseases all at once!

In light of all of this, I wonder: Is a meaningful life all about stacking up more years? Does our planet really need more human beings? Only time (and maybe this extended time) will tell if such an increase in our longevity is worthwhile.

## The Top Five Regrets of Those Dying

An oft-cited survey was conducted a year ago by a hospice nurse who interviewed thousands of people at the end of their lives. She found these were the top five regrets of the dying:

- I wish I'd had the courage to live a life true to myself, not the life others expected of me. (Most common)
- I wish I hadn't worked so hard. (Most men)
- I wish I'd had the courage to express my feelings.
- I wish I had stayed in touch with my friends.
- I wish that I had let myself be happier.

There was no mention of more sex or bungee jumps.

Another list of five that I often cite is from David Richo's book *The Five Things We Cannot Change and the Happiness We Find in Embracing Them.*

When discussing the consideration of making life-or-death decisions, he says there are five basic truths we cannot change:

- Everything changes and ends. (Indeed, can you believe that even space and time will end?)
- Things do not always go according to plan.
- Life is not always fair.
- Pain is part of life.
- People are not loving and loyal all the time.

While I am neither a pessimist nor one who believes that one must simply bear suffering no matter how severe, I do find it sometimes helpful to remember these truths. And I wish someone had explained these realities to me while I was still in elementary school!

Meanwhile, to learn more about death and dying issues, you may want to find your nearest Death Café (*deathcafe.com*). At a Death Café, people, often strangers, gather to eat cake, drink tea, and discuss death in a relaxed and safe, non-judgmental environment. The objective is to increase awareness of death with a view toward helping people make the most of their finite lives. There are no other agendas, objectives or themes. It is a discussion group rather than a grief support or counseling session. Death Cafés are always offered on a not-for-profit basis, in an accessible, respectful and confidential space and with no intention of leading people to any conclusion, product, or course of action. I often hear people say, "Time heals all." I say, "Not just time, but time and what you do with it."

Finally, a few more quotations:

> The rare opportunity to exist, no matter how brief, is worth the pain left in the wake of its disappearance.
>
> — Chris Matakas, *Human: Learning To Live In Modern Times*

> Like I said, Kenzie. Everything ends. "I'm not afraid to die," you say with a wan smile. "I just hope I'm smart enough to stay dead."
>
> — Victoria Schwab, *The Archived*

> That's the secret. If you always make sure you're exactly the person you hoped to be, if you always make sure you know only the very best people, then you won't care if you die tomorrow.
>
> — Carol Rifka Brunt, *Tell the Wolves I'm Home*

May you live life with as few regrets as possible. And if you care to raise a glass, I leave you with one of my favorite toasts: "May you live as long as you want to, and want to as long as you live!"

# Epilogue
# Death and Humor

*Evil prevails where laughter is not known.*

— an Inuit saying

It may seem incongruous to link death with humor, but I believe it is worth the effort. You've undoubtedly heard someone say, "I didn't know whether to laugh or cry." Maybe we can do both.

In case my description of how death can be a gift to life in Chapter 7 is not enough to help soften the hard subject of death and dying, here are some musings about humor and death for your delectation. I hope you find this to be jocund and that this renders you to be sufficiently gruntled.

## Jest Death

My Laughing Skull

*I, of course, hope to die just like my Grandfather: peacefully in my sleep. Not crying and screaming like the passengers in his car!*

At the outset, I apologize in advance for offending anyone. Many jokes are told at someone's expense, often lampooning. Although I have tried to be careful, there is usually a group or someone who is the "butt" of the joke. So, please don't take it personally.

Many jokes commonly told are tasteless. They do not make me laugh — they're even repulsive, gruesome, grotesque. Yet I think it can be useful to look at those, because they are told. You remember, for example the tragedy of January, 1986 when the space shuttle Challenger blew up, killing seven astronauts? Of course, the death of those seven astronauts was not funny.

But I cannot tell you how many kids I heard tell one another Challenger jokes after that. Things like: What does NASA stand for? "Need Another Seven Astronauts." Needless to say, those kinds of jokes are out there, along with other repulsive jokes about people with disabilities, ethnic groups, etc. I do not value those kinds of jokes, though I am convinced it can be useful to examine them.

I remind you again that the dying person has a sense of humor, as I discussed earlier with reference to the quote from the movie *One Flew Over The Cuckoo's Nest*: "Man, when you lose your laugh, you lose your footing." I would hope that those of us who work with loss would take heed to those words of the wonderfully crazy Randle Patrick McMurphy.

Be it the evil of McMurphy's hellacious institutionalization or otherwise, the holy and the humor go hand in hand. It is with this spirit of gaining a footing in life, even in the spirit of combating that which would deny life, that I speak of humor and death-related matters.

This presentation is biased pro-humor. That is, I'm speaking of what I regard as some of the potential benefits of humor, even though not all attempts at humor are good. Humor can serve to avoid subjects in an unhealthy way, and it frequently perpetuates stereotypes, like Polish jokes or such nonsense as that. Humor is often a put-down, jokes being told at someone's expense. Humor can also serve to alienate, or embarrass, or offend.

The worst instances of offense are when jokes are told that target and stereotype groups of people that the joke-teller is not part of. If you are, say, African-American, or Jewish, or Irish, or gay, or disabled, for example, you can probably get away with telling jokes that would be inappropriate for others to tell.

So, the context of humor is important. My final caution is that humor can serve to trivialize that which is actually quite important.

Having said that, this then is an advocacy of humor in death-related situations. I shall touch on ten aspects of humor. I have alliterated these just to have fun with words. Why ten? I don't know. It is a nice round number. You know, like the Ten Commandments, or, if you are an Episcopalian, those are known as the "ten suggestions." As an Episcopal priest, maybe I can get away with saying that!

## The Ten Aspects of Humor

### 1. Raising by Remarking

I would maintain that at least humor raises something into our consciousness by remarking on the topic — something that may not otherwise be there. Humor may serve to articulate that which is ineffable, that which is beyond words. Many jokes are about sex. Why? Because we cannot really describe sex. Really, try explaining to someone what your last orgasm was like. Any honest effort is likely to sound humorous to others.

The point is that talking around death is still to mention death. Some examples: We're all familiar with many euphemisms for "death" as I mentioned earlier. Even to use those euphemisms is at least to acknowledge that death has taken place.

An example is the joke about the captain who approaches the sergeant and says: "Sergeant, we've just gotten word that Smith's grandmother died, and you need to go break the news to him." The sergeant walks into the barracks and pauses at the doorway and shouts "Hey, Smith, your grandmother died." Well, the captain is horrified, saying "Sergeant, that's not the way you tell a man his grandmother just died! Look at how you have shocked him! We're going to send you to tact and diplomacy school!" Well, the sergeant spent a full year, on our government nickel, at tact and diplomacy school. Upon his return the captain approached him and asked how he did. "Very well," was the reply. "That's great" said the captain, "because we just got word that Lopez's grandfather died, and you need to let him know." The sergeant goes to the barracks and calls all his men to attention in a straight line in front of him and says: "All those with living grandfathers, take one step forward! — Not so fast, Lopez!" Pretty tactful, don't you think?

There may be no good way to give bad news. It may sometimes be helpful to talk around it — a way to mention the unmentionable. But death can be impossible to describe, and it may leave us virtually speechless. Words are not enough. That is often the case in terms of the awkwardness I feel when confronted with the indescribability of death. I mean, how many times following a death have you said and heard others say, "I just don't know what to say." There's a reason for that. The many euphemisms we use to describe the death event are better than no mention whatsoever.

Just as the staples of comedy are sex and body waste, so death may be included with these unmentionables. Through comedy, attention is directed to these particulars of every-day life: sex, body waste, and death. Now, a more heroic sophistication would be ready to dress those up, cover them up, forget about them, and otherwise treat them as unmentionable. I think, for instance, of nervous laughter. The nervous laughter happens when it is a subject we're a little bit afraid to address. But at least in doing so, laughing nervously, the subject is before us: it is within our consciousness. Yes, we may not be too comfortable, we don't know quite how to talk about it, but it's there — it's a start.

Another dimension of raising up by remarking is that humor can serve to lift us up. It may help us feel better about ourselves. In paying attention to these unmentionables, comedy is uplifting. Classic tragedy, on the other hand (Shakespeare's and others), terminates in death and destruction. Comedy ends in life and reunion. Comedy itself may be considered a force against the finality of death in this regard. The comedy puts things back together. It ends in a feast, a marriage, a celebration, and an upbeat mood. The tragedy *Hamlet*, for example, achieves multiple funerals in the end, whereas Shakespeare's *As You Like It* culminates in a quadruple wedding. These sorts of endings in "happily ever after" or paradise-like fairy-tale ways are uplifting. Comedy may do this with a knowing wink or a nodding smile, knowing it's too good to be true, but at least it's fun. While it may describe a sort of fairy tale that does not really happen, at least it is uplifting and raises the spirit.

**2. Lovingly Linked**

Humor provides fellowship; it is relational. A joke along these lines is about the two fellows who love baseball, Fred and Bob. Fred dies and Bob is bereft. One of Bob's great wonders is, "Well, gee, is there baseball in heaven?" If Fred were playing baseball in heaven Bob sure would like to know. Well, Fred reappears one day from heaven to his buddy Bob. Bob, of course, is delighted to hear from him and says, "Tell me, Fred! Is there baseball in heaven?" Fred says, "I have good news and I have bad news. The good news is yes, we have baseball in heaven. The bad news is, you're pitching tomorrow."

The point being that we're all in this together. It's a less threatening way to say, "You, Bob, are going to die too." The mention of mortality can be a source of unity and fellowship. Comedy serves to unite people, thereby overcoming loneliness, alienation, isolation, and estrangement. Comedy also breaks down inhibitions. It engenders a feeling of "we're all in it together" as does recognizing the universality of death, if you will.

Take the fun-filled game we play with infants: peek-a-boo. We disappear and we reappear. When we come back the infant's little face lights up and the eyes sparkle, and there is a smile. Consider this first explicitly human response of a lifetime: the smile, when that tiny little face lights up. It may be timid at first, but it is the beginning of the breakthrough of communication: the smile. Shortly after comes laughter. Granted that crying unites us also, and maybe at an earlier stage than laughing, but crying unites many animals. Smiling, as far as I can tell, seems to be unique to humans.

Unity and fellowship are important for the caregiver also. Hey, we're all in this together too. It is important to be able to joke with one another, particularly those of us who face high-stress situations involving matters of life and death. An example of this is the story I told earlier about the state hospice meeting years ago when, at the dinner banquet, we all stood up and told limericks, poking fun at ourselves, our patients, and our work. It was outrageous and funny. There was a great sense of camaraderie and esprit-de-corps as those limericks were told. It was a relief of tension and a reminder that we were all in it together, and at least let us have a good laugh. Now, granted, the outsider may have taken a dim view of some of the jokes we made about death and patients, but it was important for ourselves to lighten up.

Comedy is also meant to unite by its very nature. And it is meant to encourage others. Think about this: you need more than one person to tell a joke. I have never told myself a joke that made me laugh! You don't tell a joke to yourself. Fellowship is inherent. So we are lovingly linked.

### 3. Raucously Remembered

An example would be the time when I attended a death conference and I had a fellow come up to me whom I did not remember. He remembered me from a year and a half ago at a conference in Chicago and he said, "You're the guy who rode back with us in the cab after we had all gone to dinner. There were about eight of us in a taxi cab, and you were the one who told the joke about Abe and Sarah."

My point is that this fellow remembered me because of the humorous event. We remember comedic events. The mourning process fits here. Again, the mourning process is having the deceased go from being a presence to a memory. This process can well be facilitated by the memorable nature of humorous events. Survivors remember and recall the silly, the foolish, the stupid, the embarrassing moments and situations lived by the deceased. While possible shame, guilt or tension in this area is vented, so, too, the fools we make of ourselves are remembered. The funny times are peak experiences, which stand out vividly and are endearingly remembered.

### 4. Jest Truth Told

One example is: "You know it's a bad day when you call the suicide prevention center and they put you on hold." Another example is the story of a rancher whose horse kicked his mother-in-law to death. A large crowd turned out for the funeral. The minister says, "This lady must have been mighty popular for so many people to take off work and come to here for the funeral." "They're not here for the funeral," the rancher said, "these people are here to buy the horse!"

Truth is told in death–related jokes. Humor enables us to speak some harsh truth, some helpful truth, which would otherwise be untold. Not every crisis is readily resolved (we are put on hold), and we say so in a less threatening way with humor. Likewise: Yes, sometimes we may wish our mother-in-law were no longer around. A less threatening way to say so is a way to laugh instead of becoming outraged or angry about our predicament.

In fact, sometimes we'd like to kill others! I remember reading Saul Bellows' book *Hertzog* about fifty-three years ago, in which he said, "It is natural to wish a death a day." That was liberating to me, not that I am a nasty guy, but those thoughts do sometimes occur — that one's life would be easier if a certain other person did not exist.

Back to the topic — The fool, along with other comic figures, is a reminder of the essential true awkwardness of the human situation. James Sulley says, "While satire, sarcasm, and their kind seem to be trying to push things away or at least to alter them, humor, curiously enough, looks as if it were tenderly holding to the very world which entertains it." And I would submit that humor holds to the world and then interprets the world for us by telling us some truth.

One of the saving attributes of human nature is that we may see humor in things great and small, able to laugh and to joke at all of life. Humor takes on feast and famine, funerals and weddings. It encounters all of life with a note of hope. The classic clown, Emmett Kelley, the hobo who never had good luck, exemplifies one of the truths told. He always got the short end of the stick but he kept on trying. The comic bounces back, again testifying to the truth of resiliency of the human spirit.

Life also is not predictable, as those of us who work with death certainly know. Life is, indeed, fragile. Comedy comes directly to terms with the arbitrary nature of life.

### 5. Common Conundrum

Comedy, like death itself, is the great leveler. It renders us all equal, like the story about the bank president I cited earlier in Chapter 11.

Just as humor raises up the meek or the lowly, so too it takes down the high and mighty, namely in this case the doctor in our society where the punchline in the joke about the bank president concludes with Saint Peter saying, "That's no doctor, that's God. He just likes to play doctor sometimes!" It renders us equal.

Comedy also is the protagonist of all that is natural, however ordinary or lowly. It is the antagonist of all that is unnatural, artificial, affected or pretentious. It is a kind of faith in what is the essential goodness of persons, not just debunking. So comedy celebrates what is natural to humankind. It glorifies all appearances of being human and it points to lesser losses than death. The grand human menagerie struts its stuff on the stage of humor. Granted we are each unique, but we are all the same as human beings.

### 6. Release and Relief

The joke here might be the story of Sarah and Abe. Sarah and Abe know that Abe is almost on the verge of death. They are doing some life recollection, some remembering, sitting on their rocking chairs on the front porch. Abe says to Sarah, "You remember when we first got married thirty years ago and I sold everything I had and I took my last penny to buy our home for us and then it burned down. And you were with me, Sarah. You were there." And

Sarah says, "Yes Abe. I remember and I was with you." A few quiet moments pass and Abe goes on to say, "And Sarah, you remember after that, when I took the insurance money from the home and invested it in the restaurant business and we went bankrupt? And you were with me Sarah, you were there with me." And Sarah says, ""Yes Abe, I remember. I was there. I was with you."

And this goes on in a similar vein with stories of disappointment and failure and after the last time Abe says, "You were with me Sarah. You were there through it all." Sarah again confirms, "Yes Abe, I was with you." Abe turns to Sarah and says, "Sarah, you're just a jinx!" It relieves tension, frustration. Comedy can be release and relief. In this case perhaps even relieving anger.

Humor is a safety valve for the release, relief and discharge of tense emotion. In cutting through the discomforting experience, humor may purge us. I think again, for instance, of a funeral (true story). I presided at a funeral and the survivors, the family, were seated aside together but there was some confusion as to who would be sitting where. They changed seats a couple of times and someone in the group remarked, "Gee, here it is a funeral and we're playing musical chairs!" The comment didn't engender raucous laughter, but it served to break the tension.

Feelings expressed through laughter dissipate anxiety. The tears of good laughter are beneficial, as are the tears of grief. We feel better after a good laugh. It is cathartic to chuckle. Comedy is concerned with relieving and moderating tensions, not with supercharging them. Flexibility is, after all, the characteristic of life, while rigidity is the sign of death.

### 7. Dodge and Deny

As an example, take the story I told earlier about the little boy whose cat dies and does not understand why the cat had to die. His mother explains that God wanted the cat, leading the boy to wonder why God would want a dead cat. That is an example of dodging, changing the perception of a situation. Things are turned around. Here we have the same circumstances. The cat is still dead but we can laugh instead of cry.

Humor may serve as an escape, to distract, to defend, or to numb in a healthy, helpful way. Just as one no more looks steadily at death than at the sun, so comedy might protect us. It's a shield from death's harshness — dodge and deny. Situations are not changed but their perceptions are.

Humor may let us escape in another way. In the drift of comedy no one gets seriously hurt. Cream pies are hurled, not nuclear missiles. Serious conflict is transformed into sport or rivalry. I think, for instance, of post-war comedies like *Sergeant Bilko, McHale's Navy, Hogan's Heros, Gomer Pyle,*and *M*A*S*H*. There may be bluffs and fisticuffs, but there is not deadly power out of all proportion to the need to defend territory, or obtain food, or protect one's self. Like Don Quixote, the comic, as opposed to tragic hero, may take on a windmill or two, but he is not eager to die or to kill others. Comedy is committed to life, to saving skin, and not to saving face. Comedy defends the person, not the principle — the spirit, not the law. Humor may even mitigate war. Such reversal and dodging and denying are constructive roles.

### 8. Competing Complexities and Contradictions

An example is the suicide note:

> Dear Mother,
> I hate you.
> Love, Susan

The competing emotions are love and hate. In the process of mourning as a path to recovering equilibrium, humor allows competing emotions to be expressed. "I didn't know whether to laugh or cry." Maybe the bereft could do either.

Another example: generally speaking, even someone who is dearly loved, as deceased, may yet be the target of anger, with feelings of abandonment or feeling cheated, or anger about other matters. We live in a world where we usually speak better of the dead than of the living. Think about whom we call "Loved Ones" — it's usually the dead. It is not okay to speak ill of the deceased. Yet we have those mixed emotions.

Uncertainty and ambiguity are acceptable, says humor. Comedy counterbalances in this way. It tames the beast or it ties down the angel in us. In this same vein, comedy is a moderator of passions. Humor brings about wholeness in enabling a unity of the self.

In the history of the comedic tradition, something holy is profane and something profane is made holy. Customary expectations are overturned and established categories are jumbled or reversed.

### 9. Laughter Liberates

Humor gives freedom as it liberates us from convention, turning us back into an appreciation of everyday life. A story here is one about the woman who complained that she could never get caught up. Every day for twenty years she looked at her desk piled high with unfinished matters and letters and bills and so on, and appointments — she could never get caught up. And when she left her desk, she walked out of the house to get away from the clutter. There was still the grass that needed to be cut, and the hedges had to be trimmed. If only she could once get caught up.

Then she had a dream. She dreamed that in the next life she was in a large room with a beautiful desk, clean, clear, and shiny. There were no appointments, nothing on the desk. Through the window she could see the neatly manicured lawn. It was a relief: she had caught up. Thank the Lord. Or was it good? All around the edge of this paradise there nibbled a little question: "What do I do now?" There was nothing to do. And one day the mailman came down the street just whistling. The mailman had no letters for our woman. He was just out for a walk. "Please tell me" the woman said, "What place is this?" "Why, don't you know?" replied the mailman cheerily. "This is hell."

What do you do if you have nothing to do? Humor says that the ordinariness of life is okay. And such insight can be liberating. Those of us who work with death already have a great appreciation of life. Our interest in death is an interest in life. Nevertheless, comedy frees us by reawakening us to a new zest for life. We as humans search for meaning and purpose, and sometimes encounter disenchantment or restlessness, which may be overcome by comedy.

Through comedy we may appreciate life and what we have rather than wishing to have more — or larger or bigger or better.

Comedy is the world of energy going nowhere in particular but enjoying the going. It makes us glad to be alive. Giggling, wiggling, teasing, wondering, thoroughly in the present moment.

Through comedy, things begin to jump out at us, to strike us, to hit us as peculiar, incredible, and in their own right fantastic. Jokes have a punch line, a twist. The surprise tells us we are alive, rejoicing therein. With humor we are free to reawaken to the intrinsic meaning and value we find in the simplest or most familiar things. A brush with death will have the same effect.

Many television sitcoms fit this category. Another example is the final seconds of Charlie Chaplin's film *The Tramp*. At the end he kicks up his heels and he walks jauntily away, exhibiting the courage and the transformation yielded by comedy. We are free to recognize that the truly human spirit is there all along, able to rise above the ups and downs of life's vicissitudes. On the one hand it lifts us and transcends the muck of ordinary life, yet we are free to appreciate the ordinariness that life holds for each of us.

### 10. Humor Humbles

It is important not to take ourselves too seriously. Example: Woody Allen's joke about the fellow on the verge of death and someone else's life flashes before his eyes. What does that say? It says, "Hey, who are you after all? What makes you so important? Or, who am I, John Abraham?" Humor keeps us humble.

Another example is the joke of the caregiver who has never been with a person at the point of death and is eager to do so for the learning experience. At last the caregiver is in the hospital room, standing next to the man who is about to die and the man is gasping and struggling, drugged and plugged, with tubes in his throat. He cannot speak but wants to write a note. He manages to write a note to the caregiver and just as he hands it to her he dies. There is a great deal of commotion. The staff come rushing into the room and the caregiver is asked to leave. As she does so, at least she says to herself, "Well, I've got his last words here in this note." Alas, the note says: "You are standing on my oxygen hose!"

Sure. We all make mistakes and this is a less threatening way to say so. Humor humbles us. In fact, one of my favorite leadership phrases is: "Let's go make a mistake together." And one of my favorite prayers: "Oh God of the second chance, it's me again!"

Another example is a true story of a funeral I did as an Episcopal priest. I thought I had done an excellent job. I do not always preach at funerals, but I preached at this one. I did a great piece of death work and I had been with the family throughout this man's terrible demise. Afterward it was promptly called to my attention that the only name I had mentioned, other than the deceased, during the funeral (and I should add that the other names all deserved to be mentioned) was "Maggie," the family dog. Their comments, made in good humor, humbled me.

Those of us in this field, who of course deal with death better than anyone else (wink), might want to remind ourselves of our frailties and limitations.

A writer was complaining recently in a Christian magazine that jokes were sometimes made about Christianity on television, as if Christians could not be funny, or were somehow sacrosanct. Well, I do not buy that. The more we laugh at ourselves the better, no matter what one's religious beliefs may be. Even in such weighty a matter as death or death-related work, the more we laugh, the better, including at ourselves. How else can we encounter our inflationary tendencies, our notion of being extra-special or better. After all, as I say, not everyone comes to grips with death as well as we.

Along these lines there is a Hasidic story of a pious Jew who launched into a doleful jeremiad to a holy man, saying, "I have labored hard and long in the service of the Lord and yet I have received no improvement. I am still an ordinary and ignorant person." The Baalshem, the holy man, responded, "Ah, but you have gained the realization that you are ordinary and ignorant." I would bet the pious Jew was not very grateful. But this can be a healthy realization.

Finally, I conclude with this: In the comic vision, the meaning of life is within itself. In the comic vision the purpose of life is fundamentally to live. Rather like the dance. The purpose of dancing is not to get from point A to point B on the dance floor. The purpose of dancing is to dance. So I hope with humor, we might have the same end — simply to laugh and to enjoy life. Find life as it is and rejoice in it. Let us laugh, merely enjoying the laughter. And, just for some more chuckles:

A cartoonist was found dead in his home. Details are sketchy.

When chemists die, they barium.

Don't worry about old age; it doesn't last.

# Appendix A

# A Day to be Celebrated

## Death with Dignity Day Opens a Universal Conversation

by Frank Kavanaugh, Ph.D.

Rarely is a single book powerful enough to establish a new civil liberty and start a movement to create it. Such is Derek Humphry's *Final Exit*, which, in 1991, affirmed the notion that deeply ill individuals had a right to end their own suffering. The decision lay in themselves, and *Final Exit* was a how-to book.

It was privately published because no commercial publisher would touch it, and, to everyone's surprise, it flew off the shelves. It has since sold an estimated 2 million copies in the U.S. and all over the world.

Since Mr. Humphry's bold statement of belief and action, much of Western Europe and the United States is witnessing a dramatic revolution in the understanding of a dignified and peaceful death as a human liberty.

The battle for end-of-life autonomy has advanced more slowly, but it advances. Now, on the 25th anniversary of the book's publication, Jan. 2 marked Death With Dignity Day. This day of worldwide conversation supports the nameless who currently endure daily, hopeless misery, and to offer hope and peace of mind for their kindred sufferers in the future.

Such conversations most importantly begin intimately, and in your own families. You are the protagonist in your own drama. It is your words, your script, your wishes, created by your own awareness of your needs and willingness to express them, so that if you cannot speak for yourself, your children, friends and significant others will do it for you, even if they do not agree with your position.

With this ice-breaking talk on the details of your dying wishes, some important caveats cannot be ignored, and whatever kept you silent cannot do so any longer. If you would end your life on your own terms, your children must be informed, or the ripples could reach astronomic proportions.

The talk cannot be postponed for a "better" time. This time may be the best one you will have.

If at all possible, schedule a meeting in which all involved can attend. If at a public place, find a quiet corner where you can hear each other. Let them know you need to share something important.

As with any difficult communication, the first sentence is the hardest to say. Have it ready.

Talk about your personal "best possible death." What is your threshold concerning suffering? Do you want doctors to try everything possible to sustain your life or do you prefer to exit on your own terms?

You must be prepared with your Advance Directives, or Living Will, and procedures you want and those you absolutely want no part of. At the very least, include options for end-of-life care: desires for or against nursing homes, hospice, ventilation, feeding tubes, pain relief, hastened death, specific medical procedures such as resuscitation, antibiotics, etc. If doctors and hospital are posturing for a "cure" that sounds futile and contrary to your acceptance of reality, reject them — even typical procedures such as blood tests.

Many years later, when children of yours are the patients facing their own endings, they will be repeating the same concept to those assembled: "These decisions are mine — about me. They are not anyone else's to make. Your voice and will must be strong and assertive on my behalf."

You are not asking for advice, or a discussion of anything other than how to best implement your wishes. As loved ones naturally rebut your choice with "Is this is a good idea?" or "You're going to be fine," or "Let's not talk about this now," realize it's because they love you. But ask them: "Are you saying no because you love me? Do you know better than I where my best interests lie? Is it love to watch me suffer against my will?"

Discuss "good deaths" and "bad deaths," using as examples people they know or knew. If they have no experience of a bad death, bring information to the table. A justification such as "I don't want to see all I've saved for your futures go down the drain" invites attempts to veto your decision. A better discussion starts with something like this: "I love you, and you need to be clear about my wishes, so there are no guesses and no regrets."

Without this dialogue and its follow-up with medical caregivers, most people die the way they most dreaded: tethered to machines and surrounded by strangers in a hospital.

At the end of life, timidity is a luxury no one can afford. A patient has the right to refuse any and all medical procedures, but critical caregivers don't always make it easy. Thus, your advocates' voices must be loud and clear on your behalf. When your advocates say no, the staff must understand that these are your personal wishes.

If advocates run into opposition, ask for someone in authority: a supervisor, a manager, a patient representative or social worker. Call in hospice staff and hear what they have to say.

Stark reality is facing you in the mirror, and your courage is looking back at it.

The time for denial and false hope is over.

*Dr. Frank Kavanaugh serves on the boards of the Final Exit Network and the Hemlock Society of Florida. He has been a health educator for 40 years, retiring as professor of medical and public affairs at the George Washington University Medical Center and professor of communications with an endowed chair at George Washington University. He is chairman emeritus of the International Academy for Preventive Medicine and a former vice president of the Cooper Institute for Advanced Studies in Medicine and the Humanities.*

## How We Used to Die; How We Die Now

by Louis Profeta, MD

An emergency physician's beautifully written and agonizingly empathic account of "how we used to die" starkly contrasted with how most people die now in our death-defying, death-dealing military industrial medicopharmaceuticalized culture.

> In the old days, she would be propped up on a comfy pillow, in fresh clean sheets under the corner window where she would in days gone past watch her children play. Soup would boil on the stove just in case she felt like a sip or two. Perhaps the radio softly played Al Jolson or Glenn Miller, flowers sat on the night stand, and family quietly came and went. These were her last days. Spent with familiar sounds, in a familiar room, with familiar smells that gave her a final chance to summon memories that will help carry her away. She might have offered a hint of a smile or a soft squeeze of the hand but it was all right if she didn't. She lost her own words to tell us that it's OK to just let her die, but she trusted us to be her voice and we took that trust to heart.

You see, that's how people used to die. We saw our elders differently then.

We could still look at her face and deep into her eyes and see the shadows of a soft, clean, vibrantly innocent child playing on a porch somewhere in the Midwest during the 1920s perhaps. A small rag doll dances and flays as she clutches it in her hand. She laughs with her barefoot brother, who is clad in overalls, as he chases her around the yard with a grasshopper on his finger. She screams and giggles. Her father watches from the porch in a wooden rocker, laughing while mom gently scolds her brother.

We could see her taking a ride for the first time in an automobile, a small pickup with wooden panels driven by a young man with wavy curls. He smiles gently at her while she sits staring at the road ahead; a fleeting wisp of a smile gives her away. Her hands are folded in her lap, clutching a small beaded purse.

We could see her standing in a small church. She is dressed in white cotton, holding hands with the young man, and saying, "I do." Her mom watches with tearful eyes. Her dad has since passed. Her new husband lifts her across the threshold, holding her tight. He promises to love and care for her forever. Her life is enriched and happy.

We could see her cradling her infant, cooking breakfast, hanging sheets, loving her family, sending her husband off to war, and her child to school.

We could see her welcoming her husband back from battle with a hug that lasts the rest of his life. She buries him on a Saturday under an elm, next to her father. She marries off her child and spends her later years volunteering at church functions before her mind starts to fade and the years take their toll and God says, "It's time to come home."

This is how we used to see her before we became blinded by the endless tones of monitors and whirrs of machines, buzzers, buttons and tubes that can add five years to a shell of a body that was entrusted to us and should have been allowed to pass quietly propped up in a corner room, under a window, scents of homemade soup in case she wanted a sip.

You see, now we can breathe for her, eat for her, and even pee for her. Once you have those three things covered she can — instead of being gently cradled under that corner window — be placed in a nursing home and penned in a cage of bed rails and soft restraints meant to "keep her safe."

She can be fed a steady diet of Ensure through a tube directly into her stomach and she can be kept alive until her limbs contract and her skin thins so much that a simple bump into that bed rail can literally open her up, Done until her exposed tendons are staring into the eyes of an eager medical student looking for a chance to sew. She can be kept alive until her bladder is chronically infected, until antibiotic resistant diarrhea flows and pools in her diaper so much that it erodes her buttocks. The fat padding around her tailbone and hips are consumed and ulcers open up exposing the underlying bone, which now becomes ripe for infection.

We now are in a time of medicine where we will take that small child running through the yard, being chased by her brother with a grasshopper on his finger, and imprison her in a shell that does not come close to radiating the life of what she once had. We stopped seeing her, not intentionally perhaps, but we stopped.

This is not meant as a condemnation of the family of these patients or to question their love or motives, but it is meant to be an indictment of a system that now herds these families down dead-end roads and prods them into believing that this is the new norm, and that somehow the old ways were the wrong ways and this is how we show our love.

A day does not go by where my partners don't look at each other and say, "How do we stop this madness? How do we get people to let their loved ones die?"

I've been practicing emergency medicine for close to a quarter of a century now and I've cared for countless thousands of elderly patients. I, like many of my colleagues, have come to realize that while we are developing more and more ways to extend life, we have also provided water and nutrients to a forest of unrealistic expectations that have real-time consequences for those frail bodies that have been entrusted to us.

This transition to doing more and more did not just happen on a specific day in some month of some year. Our end-of-life psyche has slowly devolved and shifted and a few generations have passed since the onset of the Industrial Revolution of medicine. Now we are trapped. We have accumulated so many options, drugs, stents, tubes, FDA-approved snake oils and procedures that there is no way we can throw a blanket over all our elderly and come to a consensus as to what constitutes inappropriate and excessive care. We cannot separate out those things meant to simply prolong life from those meant to prolong quality life.

Nearly 50 percent of the elderly U.S. population now die in nursing homes or hospitals. When they do finally die, they are often surrounded by teams of us doctors and nurses, medical students, respiratory therapists and countless other health care providers pounding on their chests, breaking their ribs, burrowing large IV lines into burned-out veins and plunging tubes into swollen and bleeding airways. We never say much as we frantically try to save the life we know we can't save or perhaps silently hope we don't save. When it's finally over and the last heart beat blips across the screen and we survey the clutter of bloody gloves, wrappers, masks and needles that now litter the room, you may catch a glimpse as we bow our heads in shame, fearful perhaps that someday we may have to stand in front of God as he looks down upon us and says, "What in the hell were you thinking?"

When it comes time for us to be called home, those of us in the know will pray that when we gaze down upon our last breath we will be grateful that our own doctors and families chose to do what they should instead of what they could. With that we will close our eyes to familiar sounds in a familiar room, a fleeting smile and a final soft squeeze of a familiar hand.

*Dr. Louis M. Profeta is an emergency physician practicing in Indianapolis. He is the author of the critically acclaimed book,* The Patient in Room Nine Says He's God.

Appendix C

# A Poem About My Cupboard

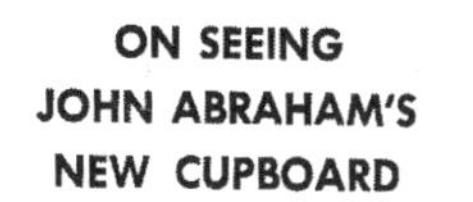

**ON SEEING JOHN ABRAHAM'S NEW CUPBOARD**

The coffin was wood,
made into a liquor cabinet for the
meantime. The advertisement,
using the voice of a preacher
man, a guru, said it would
enrich your life to be
aware that death was
always at your left
side (or was it your
right?) And be-
sides, it would
be nice to get
to know
your
final
bed.

—Judy McCallum

*Judy, the wife of a colleague of mine when I was at Saint John's Episcopal Church, Georgetown, wrote this poem after seeing my coffin at a party at my home in 1975.*

# Appendix D
# A Physician's View of Death with Dignity

## First, Do No Harm

By John Rowe III, MD, Medford, Oregon, *Journal of the American Medical Association,* September 1, 2015

Somehow, as a kid growing up in a nonreligious family, I developed a very strong sense of right and wrong, of what ethical and moral behavior should be. I have tried to follow this tenet throughout my life. When I became involved with medicine, I took to heart all the maxims we were taught, particularly "First, do no harm." But for many years now I have realized that this concept is wrong. I believe that our first duty as physicians is to relieve pain and suffering, whether it be physical or emotional. Only then, secondarily, are we to avoid harming the patient.

I say this because, as a neurologist and clinical neurophysiologist, I spent a great part of my practice causing pain and suffering in my patients, on purpose. I have performed painful electromyograms and nerve conduction studies in patients, some of whom had to stop the procedures because they could not tolerate the discomfort. I have irrigated ears to make patients vertiginous, sometimes to the point of their vomiting. I have ordered painful or dangerous diagnostic tests. The worst, before modern imaging, was the pneumoencephalogram, a truly horrific thing for any person to undergo. Arteriography occasionally resulted in catastrophic strokes. I still remember a young actor with a small subarachnoid bleed who emerged with a severe aphasia and a normal study.

I have ordered medications with, at times, seriously uncomfortable or dangerous side effects. I have recommended operations that potentially could leave patients much worse off than they were. I have caused emotional distress by discussing brain death diagnoses, terminal illness prognoses, end-of-life issues that needed addressing (i.e., a young father in denial whom I literally bullied into writing a will before he would become incompetent from his glioblastoma), limitation of driving or solo living for patients with dementia, and so on.

I have done all these things because I believed it was in each patient's best interests, to discover the cause of their problem or to alleviate their suffering, whatever form it took. These were my primary overriding concerns in all cases. First to diagnose and treat. Then, secondarily, to try to cause no unnecessary harm. The "unnecessary" being the key—synonymous with unwarranted, unjustified, inappropriate, and, if I may, merciless.

Now for the gist of where this is going. I believe wholeheartedly in assisted death. Not assisted suicide for depression. Depression is a treatable, reversible condition. Suicide is inappropriate, except in untreatable, unbearable suffering. Death is not treatable or preventable. Death can be easy or it can be utterly, devastatingly miserable. It can be totally destructive of all dignity, privacy, and autonomy, much less comfort. We have all seen it.

For years, I practiced in a state where, if someone thought you were administering too much pain medication to a terminally ill patient and the patient died, you could be charged with and possibly convicted of murder. No amount of suffering was felt justified to intervene with "natural" death. I personally have never met an individual who truly believed this on a rational, reasoned basis. In those who have professed this conviction, once the superficial logic had been taken away, it was always, at root, based on religious conviction. As such it has always been impervious to true discussion.

I fully respect the right of individuals to their own beliefs and end-of-life wishes. I do not condone the imposition of personal religious beliefs on someone who does not share the same convictions. I believe it to be morally, ethically, humanely, and mercifully unconscionable that a dying person must accept prolonged suffering if that individual does not wish it. Yet this is the law in 47 of the United States [at the time of this writing]—and the official position of the American Medical Association. This sometimes is justified by the myth that physical and emotional suffering at the end of life can be controlled. We all know that this is often not possible. Sometimes we resort finally to medicating the individual into a semiconscious state. And just what is the point of that?

Most, supposedly rational reasons against assisted death are based on the "slippery slope" concept, that it opens the door to abuse and willful murder and then eventually to euthanasia. This ignores the ability of people of intelligence and good will to write appropriate guidelines and laws to protect against such actions. Some of these people crafted the Oregon Death With Dignity Act. In this act, passed by statewide vote in 1994 and re-passed and enacted in 1997, an adult Oregon state resident with a diagnosed illness confirmed by two physicians as likely to be terminal within 6 months, who is found to be mentally competent and not significantly depressed, may be written a prescription for a lethal amount of an oral medication, which must be self-administered. Statistical, demographic, and medical data have been collected on the people who have received such prescriptions since 1997.

Obviously, there is a personal issue. Two months ago, I was diagnosed with advanced myelodysplastic syndrome. My estimated survival time is 4 to 6 months, which I suspect is optimistic. At my age, 73, and general medical condition, bone marrow transplant is not an option. Chemotherapy might offer a few months of extended existence, at the risk of spending it all sick from adverse effects. I have opted for palliative care in hospice. I will eventually die of anemia or infection of some sort.

And there is the rub. What sort of death will it be? I personally opt for as easy as possible.

*Reprinted with permission from Dr. Rowe, who has since died.*

Appendix

# A Unitarian's Essay about Avoidable Distress

# E

## Cross My Heart and Hope to Die

Doug Muder, *UU World*, February 22, 2016

When my end comes, I hope I will have the power to die well.

One day in my father's final year, he slumped to the floor while pushing his walker down a nursing home hallway. The staff came running, but he asked them not to call an ambulance. Later, when my sister wondered why, he told her, "I was hoping that was it."

That wasn't it. He lived another seven months, waiting for God to take him home and wondering what the holdup was.

Over the last five years, I've watched both my parents and my father-in-law decline and die. All three left me thinking, "That's not how I want to go."

Indeed, it could have been worse. None of the three lived the kinds of horror stories I've seen in TV dramas. Their "Do Not Resuscitate" orders were respected, so none lingered as attachments to machines. The medical system did what it could to minimize their pain rather than increase it with heroic one-last-hope treatments. But the very ordinariness of their dying process was horrifying in a different way.

I couldn't tell myself, "This is what happens when something goes terribly wrong." It just seemed to be what happens: The world shrinks, and people and places fall off the edge as you realize you will never see them again. Topics of conversation shrink as well, until even the weather becomes just another TV show — a show behind a different kind of glass.

And of course, no matter what drugs they give you, there is pain and distress. Eventually you need help to eat, help to sit in a chair, help to visit any room other than the one your bed is in. Life is full of embarrassing surprises as you lose control of bodily systems and have to wait for someone to clean you.

The most intractable pain is mental. My father-in-law developed increasingly dark delusions that could not be addressed in the reality where his daughters lived. One day he was surprised to see my wife, because he believed she was in the hospital recovering from a violent rape. Other days he waited to be arrested for the murders he believed he had committed recently, during a period when it took more than one person to get him out of bed.

I can't imagine how I would feel if I believed things like that.

And what joyful events sat in the other pan of the balance? The Stephen King line I find most terrifying is a philosophical observation made by the narrator of *Duma Key*: "Someday, if your life is long and your thinking machinery stays in gear, you'll live to remember the last good thing that ever happened to you."

I don't believe that statement is literally true; flashes of happiness can slip past even the most dismal circumstances. Still, I wonder: When will I have my last good day? How many days will come after that? As few as possible, I find myself hoping.

At the moment, I still find life fascinating, and I think of myself as a character in many stories whose endings I am curious to see. But I suspect that my world, like my parents', will shrink as my abilities diminish. I hope I will manage my retreat skillfully, that I will retain enough imagination and creativity to write myself into new stories that give me meaningful goals more suited to my powers.

But it would be arrogant to expect that I will never lose that battle. If I live long enough, someday my world will shrink to the size of a room, my field of action to a bed or a chair. If I have visitors, they will come on their schedule, not mine.

I have watched four people decline toward death. My mother-in-law, in her sixties, could imagine many things to see and do, if only she could survive. My mother, in her late eighties and in considerable pain, hung on (I believe) mainly to keep my father from being alone. In their final months, only religion kept my father and father-in-law alive. Both believed that death was God's to give, and feared that the promise of Heaven could still be revoked.

I have a different religion. I don't pretend to know what happens after death. Maybe nothing. Or if there is something, no vision of it impresses me as much more likely than the others. Maybe, as my parents believed, there is a God who will resent me interrupting his plan for my death. Or maybe the path to Heaven is tricky, so I'd best set off while I still have my wits about me.

What seems more solid to me than any such speculation is the likelihood that someday I will have wrung the last drop out of my life, and yet, perversely, I will still be alive. At that point, I have one hope left. I hope to have the power, the will, and the fortitude to toss the husk of my life aside. I hope to die. Cross my heart.

*Reprinted with Permission.*

Appendix

# The Dementia Provision

# F

Most Advance Directives become operative only when a person is unable to make health-care decisions and is either "permanently unconscious" or "terminally ill." There is usually no provision that applies to the situation in which a person suffers from severe dementia but is neither unconscious nor dying.

The following language can be added to any advance directive or living will. There it will serve to advise physicians and family of the wishes of a patient with Alzheimer's disease or other forms of dementia. You may reproduce the words below, add your signature and date, and include it with your advance directives.

> If I am unconscious and it is unlikely that I will ever become conscious again, I would like my wishes regarding specific life-sustaining treatments, as indicated on the attached additional documents of advance directives to be followed. If I remain conscious but have a progressive illness that will be fatal and the illness is in an advanced stage, and I am consistently and permanently unable to communicate, swallow food and water safely, care for myself and recognize my family and other people, and it is very unlikely that my condition will substantially improve, I would like my wishes regarding specific life-sustaining treatments, as indicated on the attached documents to be followed. If I am unable to feed myself while in this condition I do / do not (circle one) want to be fed.
>
> I hereby incorporate this provision into my durable power of attorney for health care, living will and any other previously executed advance directive for health care decisions.
>
> *To be signed and dated*

**Addition to Advance Directives:**

This directive would further recognize that I prefer dying to living in a state of dementia. When this special advance directive is triggered by the onset of dementia (at a stage in the disease discussed next, below), the first required action of caregivers would be that they not employ any of the treatments or supportive actions outlined below, which would be withheld as unwanted treatment. (Much of this list is like an ordinary living will, but not all.)

- I want no measures taken to prolong my life.
- I wish to be kept comfortable, free of pain, and maintained in a dignified state.
- I wish any medication that is used to keep me comfortable and free of pain or other distress to be in sufficient dosage that distress, physical or psychological, is relieved, even if such medication hastens my death.
- If I get an infection, do not treat it — just make me comfortable. Use no antibiotics.
- If I cannot feed myself, just leave the food for me. Do not spoon feed me or encourage me in any way to eat or drink. Do not treat dehydration with anything other than fluids offered orally, and do not try to encourage drinking beyond what I clearly desire.
- Give me no artificial feeding or hydration of any sort. I do not want a tube inserted to administer food or hydration (no intravenous fluids).
- If I cannot breathe for myself, I do not wish to be put on a ventilator. Oxygen is not to be administered other than possibly for the relief of air hunger. Low oxygen levels in the blood are not a sufficient indication for the use of oxygen.
- If my kidneys fail, I do not want dialysis.
- If I stop breathing or my heart stops beating, I do not want cardiopulmonary resuscitation.
- I want no blood transfusions.
- If I have a heart attack or stroke, do nothing to extend my life, but do provide comfort measures.
- I want no surgery unless it is absolutely necessary to control pain.

- I want no x-rays, blood tests, other laboratory tests, or invasive diagnostic procedures.
- I do not want regular vital signs to be taken, including blood pressure and temperature measurements.
- I do not want to be treated in a hospital, but wish to be made comfortable where I reside.

Below is a set of criteria defining the sort of dementia with which I would be unwilling to live and would wish further active measures to be undertaken to shorten life and the period of suffering, such as the withholding of fluid, accompanied by sedation (terminal dehydration with sedation), which would be the next step beyond withholding unwanted treatment. Such a step would be aimed at hastening death.

## Criteria With Which I Would Not Want To Continue Living

- An irreversible condition that causes severe decline in cognitive abilities.
- Inability to recognize family and those loved by me. Inability to perform ordinary functions of self-care and cleanliness.
- Inability to feed myself.
- Repeated violent or disruptive behavior.
- Disorientation or wandering off frequently.
- Chronic confusion about my situation.
- Incoherence and/or inability to communicate.
- Chronic fearfulness or frustration due to cognitive disorder.

*To be signed and dated*

# Appendix G
# Physician Aid in Dying Does Not Go Far Enough

## Derek Humphry Looks Ahead

*Final Exit Network* Newsletter, February 2016 by Derek Humphry

Final Exit Network needs to be a movement with a future, foreseeing social trends in death and dying and leading the way to achieve them. In America, we now have four states [five states as of December, 2016] with laws permitting physician-assisted suicide. Worthwhile progress, but where now for other types of suffering? Are the current laws good enough, limited as they are by political expediency?

Passing these "prescription laws" is a wonderful start but it is not the complete answer.

The future in the choice-in-dying movement lies with a deliberate widening of the scope of people for whom we will campaign publicly and whom we will include. (Europe has been ahead of us on this.)

It is time to consider more seriously offering to help persons with long-term, untreatable mental illness. Of course, such cases must be most carefully assessed, [to include] only adults who have asserted voluntarily their need for relief from lengthy, unbearable suffering.

Persons with "terminal old-age" whose advanced years and accompanying medical problems make their life no longer worth living. In Britain since 2009 there has been the Society for Old Age Rational Suicide (SOARS), run by Dr. Michael Irwin and others, which has been making a stir. If needed, SOARS takes people to Switzerland for a peaceful ending. Already Switzerland, the Netherlands, Belgium, and Luxembourg permit this broader kind of assisted dying. Careful on-the-spot research should be made on how those European countries are handling these sensitive new issues.

We should begin to argue for the current Death-with-Dignity Acts now passed in the four states to be improved. As written now, they may be politically acceptable, but evidence reveals many unsolved problems. The six-month limitation on "likely to die" should be made more realistic. We should also campaign to allow patients who cannot swallow the lethal dose to be given it by doctor injection.

We must think through and tackle the problem of when and how Alzheimer's patients and persons with long-term degenerative diseases can be helped to die if they have an advance directive.

Long-term, we should consider opening a clinic to help the sort of people I've just been talking about. Or devise an escape route to Switzerland or Colombia as they use in Germany and Britain.

*Reprinted with Permission*

# Appendix H: Let Your Wishes be Known to Your Family

## Your Doctors Have Heard You — Now for Your Kids...

by Frank Kavanaugh, Ph.D.

YOUR FINAL, CHALLENGING COMMUNICATIONS ARE not yet completed even after you've clued in your physicians with your needs and plans.

There remains another, of equal or more importance than the first: having "that" conversation with your adult children. For those of you for whom this talk will be the first of its kind, you have an especially daunting task. There are some important caveats that cannot be ignored.

Whatever has held you back from broaching this subject with them before cannot do so any longer. If you would end your life on your own terms, your children must be informed, or the ripples can reach tsunamic proportions.

Cut the rationalizations for postponement: There is no "better" time. This time may be the best one you will have.

Plan to meet all together, adults only, in a quiet place where you can hear each other without interruptions. Let them know that this is a most important conversation, and you need everybody on board. (A restaurant is a possible place, with a quiet corner and subdued music. It is important that everyone be able to hear and see everyone else. Body language and facial expression often communicate more than words.)

As with any difficult communication, the first sentence is the hardest! Have it ready. Perhaps start by stating that you are here to share your decisions concerning what for you is a "good death" or a "bad death," and ask those present to classify examples of such passings for people they have known.

Prerequisite to your discussion is having completed your ADs and decided which medical procedures are acceptable to you and which are not. What is your personal threshold concerning suffering? Under what circumstances do you want your suffering to end? Should the staff err on the side of trying "everything" — which is endless — or providing the setting for a peaceful death? Do you want sedation?

Your children must have made themselves absolutely familiar with every wish you've expressed in those documents.

Some statements on your part are no-no's, which automatically guarantee a response that sabotages the talk. Your question, "Is this discussion a good idea?" invites, "No, it isn't," followed by all kinds of reasons: "Let's not talk about it," or, "Oh, you'll live forever, Dad, or, "You're going to be just fine," or "TMI" (Too Much Information), "or "Maybe a cure will come up!" are brush-offs that will, if you enable them, end the honesty. Avoid also the talk of being a burden and throwing too much money into a bottomless pit. Those will likely invite obligatory reassurance by your children not to do this for their sake; they'd "rather have you around."

You might ask them if that means that your indescribable misery and suffering would be OK with them. "Do you want me to die the way most people dread, tethered to machines and surrounded by strangers in a hospital, terrified? Does loving me mean that you know better than I myself what my needs and wants are? Do those statements sound like 'love' to you?"

If they offer or reiterate advice, do not respond. Repeat the same sentence: "This is my decision to make, and I have done so."

"What I want from you is support. That means that you will honor my wishes, be my mouthpiece if I can't be my own, no matter what your opinion. Perhaps that is the clearest indication of what genuine love looks like: honoring another's crucial decisions even though yours would be different."

Questions may be acceptable if their intent is clarification, not debate.

Then, ideally, your monologue opens into a specific kind of dialogue. The room is filled with loved ones who have intensive feelings about what they've just heard: fear, sadness, despair.... They need to express them and to know you care. They can do both without negating your instructions.

You want them to share their feelings, not their opinions. It is crucial that they know the difference. "I feel that you are being selfish" is not a feeling. It's a judgment. "I am upset and angry with you" is.

You cannot solve their feelings nor change them, not then. Just listening in itself does wonders. And the best response on your part is often delivered in silence: a long and loving hug. Maybe even a group hug, if it's real.

You have a wonderful opportunity in this experience to create something magical. And know that when you're coming from love, you almost can't get it wrong.

*Frank Kavanaugh serves on the boards of the Final Exit Network and the Hemlock Society of Florida. He has been a health educator for 40 years, retiring as professor of medical and public affairs at the George Washington University Medical Center and professor of communications with an endowed chair at George Washington University. He is chairman emeritus of the International Academy for Preventive Medicine and a former vice president of the Cooper Institute for Advanced Studies in Medicine and the Humanities.*

# Appendix I
# Statement by Desmond Tutu

*"Dying people should have the right to choose how and when they leave Mother Earth."*

THROUGHOUT MY LIFE, I HAVE been fortunate to have spent my time working for dignity for the living. I have campaigned passionately for people in my country and the world over to have their God-given rights.

I have been fortunate to have long spent my time working for dignity for the living. Now, as I turn 85 Friday, with my life closer to its end than its beginning, I wish to help give people dignity in dying. Just as I have argued firmly for compassion and fairness in life, I believe that terminally ill people should be treated with the same compassion and fairness when it comes to their deaths. Dying people should have the right to choose how and when they leave Mother Earth. I believe that, alongside the wonderful palliative care that exists, their choices should include a dignified assisted death.

There have been promising developments as of late in California and Canada, where the law now allows assisted dying for terminally ill people, but there are still many thousands of dying people across the world who are denied their right to die with dignity. Two years ago, I announced the reversal of my lifelong opposition to assisted dying in an op-ed in the *Guardian*. But I was more ambiguous about whether I personally wanted the option, writing: "I would say I wouldn't mind." Today, I myself am even closer to the departures hall than arrivals, so to speak, and my thoughts turn to how I would like to be treated when the time comes. Now more than ever, I feel compelled to lend my voice to this cause.

I believe in the sanctity of life. I know that we will all die and that death is a part of life. Terminally ill people have control over their lives, so why should they be refused control over their deaths? Why are so many instead forced to endure terrible pain and suffering against their wishes?

I have prepared for my death and have made it clear that I do not wish to be kept alive at all costs. I hope I am treated with compassion and allowed to pass on to the next phase of life's journey in the manner of my choice.

*Desmond Tutu, a Nobel Peace laureate, is archbishop emeritus of Cape Town, South Africa. He released this public statement on October 6, 2016.*

# Appendix J
# Inter/Met Seminary

This is not especially relevant to achieving a good death, though it is death-related since it was a great enterprise that, regrettably, died. Because I thought the concept of Inter/Met was tremendous and I greatly value the work of Dr. Fletcher, I want to elaborate a bit on the anecdote in Chapter 2 about the opening of the movie *One Flew Over the Cuckoo's Nest.* John Fletcher was a former professor and friend of mine, and brother of Louise Fletcher, the notorious Nurse Ratched in the movie. Hence my connection to it. And I had raised tens of thousands of dollars for the school.

Inter/Met Seminary was a school ahead of its time in that it educated students from all religious faiths and the students uniquely contracted with professors to be taught what the students themselves decided they needed to learn. Its first class of twenty students was open to Protestants, Jews and Roman Catholics, whites and blacks, women as well as men. This approach to training pastoral ministers turned traditional seminary concepts upside-down.

The term Inter/Met stood for Inter-faith Metropolitan Theological Education, Inc. It was set up as an experiment in theological education and was conceived by John Caldwell Fletcher, an Episcopal Priest and associate professor of church and society at Virginia Theological Seminary. Inter/Met began its pilot year in 1970–1971. Fletcher served as director. Inter-Met was founded on the premise that although the parish congregation is still the heart of religious life, the seminaries have great difficulty in preparing clergy to deal with the real strains, pressures and social issues raised out of the life of the congregation they are asked to lead. The new seminary's vision called for learning pastoral ministry in the place of ministry, that is, the churches, and not in the cloister of a seminary. It stressed residentiary theological education, but resident in the actual place of ministry.

"The educational philosophy of a seminary is that you build a pastoral experience on top of an academic foundation, " said the Rev. Dr. John Fletcher. "What we are trying to do is to build an academic competence on top of a foundation of experience in the congregation." Fletcher served as director from 1970 until 1977, and was assisted in his work by the Rev. Tilden Hampton Edwards III, director of the Washington Metropolitan Ecumenical Training Center. Tilden was also a personal friend and mentor of mine and to this day I value his book about meditation: *Living Simply Through The Day*. Unfortunately, Inter/Met ceased to exist on June 30, 1977, due to a lack of funding.

The school's philosophy made a lot of sense to me, and I regret it could not continue due to the lack of funding. It failed largely because no entity felt ownership of it. For instance, schools like Virginia Theological Seminary receive considerable financial support from Episcopal congregations and Episcopal Dioceses and would likely not survive without such backing. But because Inter/Met was interfaith, such institutions did not have a great enough stake in it to provide funding.

Appendix

# Some Research about "Good Death" K

Several different studies are cited here, including those of Dr. I. Epstein, The Institute of Medicine, Karen Kehl, the *Journal of the American Geriatrics Society*, the Veterans Affairs Medical Center, the *Annals of Internal Medicine*, Psychiatrist Dr. Ton Vink, and the *British Medical Journal*. In short, these and other findings provide evidence, internationally and fairly universally, similar agreed-upon criteria for what constitutes a good death. Some of these criteria include: no suffering, being prepared, having control, and the support of loved ones. What I find most significant about such research is the stark contrast to the way most of us die these days. Comments like "Hospitals cannot help with most of these things" and "Unfortunately, most patients do not see their wishes fulfilled" and "Decisions not previously discussed usually had to be made during a crisis" pretty well sum up our plight.

These are some of the studies that have helped established this.

I. Epstein, Ph.D., is Professor of Applied Social Work Research (Health & Mental Health) at Hunter College, New York. He presented his findings at the conference of the World Federation of Right to Die Societies which I attended in 2014. Records of deceased cancer patients between 2003 and 2005 in a palliative care unit were the sole data source.

Good death was operationally defined as the patient's record indicating no pain (physical) or anxiety (psychological), and having open and honest communication with family (social) in the final assessment by the Support Team Assessment Schedule (STAS) just before death. Using these criteria, only about one-fifth of patients (21.5%; 137 out of 638) experienced a good death. A dismal proportionate result, don't you think?

Those with a good death were significantly older and were in palliative care longer. Their records also indicated lower levels of constipation, insomnia, oral discomfort, and family anxiety at their first and at their final STAS assessments. Good death was positively associated with recorded indicators of fullness in life, caregivers' acceptance and support, and negatively with reported feelings of upset about changes in the course of their illness. The results heighten awareness among social workers and other healthcare professionals about the value of good death in patients in palliative care. This empirically-based awareness can foster professionals' ability to set intervention objectives to help patients in palliative care achieve this universally accepted goal.

These interviews yielded seven elements of good death, they are:

1. awareness of dying;
2. maintenance of hope;
3. freedom from pain and suffering;
4. sense of personal control;
5. maintenance of social connectedness;
6. preparation for departure; and
7. a sense of completion and of the timing of one's death.

More findings come from a 1997 report of The Institute of Medicine (IOM), which defined a decent or good death as one that is: free from avoidable distress and suffering for patients, families, and caregivers; in general accord with patients' families' wishes; and reasonably consistent with clinical, cultural, and ethical standards. Factors important for a good death included:

- Control of symptoms
- Preparation for death
- Opportunity for closure or "sense of completion" of the life
- Good relationship with healthcare professionals

The study says that a central concept to a "good" death is one that allows a person to die on his or her own terms relatively pain-free with dignity. An *appropriate death* is often considered to be one that occurs naturally and in old age, one that follows the natural order of things; e.g., older members die before younger ones. Perhaps the best definition of an *appropriate death* is a death that someone might choose for him or herself if presented with the choice.

That there is a yearning among ordinary patients to have more peaceful deaths has been echoed in the research of University of Wisconsin-Madison nursing professor Karen Kehl. In an article called "Moving Toward Peace: An Analysis of the Concept of a Good Death," Kehl analyzed a collection of relevant articles and, based on their contents, ranked the attributes of an ideal death as follows: "being in control, being comfortable, having a sense of closure, having one's values affirmed, trusting in care providers, and recognizing impending death." Hospitals cannot help with most of these things. Unfortunately, most patients do not see their wishes fulfilled.

Another 1998 study published in the *Journal of the American Geriatrics Society* looked at Medicare patients and found that, while most said they preferred to die at home, most died in hospitals.

Another study was conducted by Dr. Karen E. Steinhauser and colleagues at the Veterans Affairs Medical Center in Durham, N.C., who examined the constituents of a good death for patients, their families and health care providers. The eighty-five study participants had no trouble describing a "bad death" as having inadequately treated pain while receiving aggressive but futile cure-directed therapy. Patients felt disregarded, family members felt perplexed and concerned about suffering, and providers felt out of control and feared that they were not providing good care. Decisions not previously discussed usually had to be made during a crisis. Families unprepared for what happens when death is imminent often panicked and rushed the patient to the hospital, where last-ditch and usually futile attempts at resuscitation were made, when both patient and family would have preferred a home death.

A study described in *The Annals of Internal Medicine* of May 16, 2000, identified six components of a good death:

- Pain and symptom management. Pain, more so than dying itself, is too often the cause of acute anxiety among patients and their families.
- Clear decision making. Patients want to have a say in treatment decisions.
- Preparation for death. Patients want to know what to expect as their illness progresses and to plan for what will follow their deaths.
- Completion. This includes reviewing one's life, resolving conflicts, spending time with family and friends, and saying good-bye.
- Contribution to others — Many people nearing death achieve a clarity as to what is really important in life and want to share that understanding with others.
- Affirmation — Study participants emphasized the importance of being seen as a unique and whole person and being understood in the context of their lives, values and preferences.

When attending a conference of the World Federation of Right to Die Societies I heard a talk by Dutch Psychiatrist Dr. Ton Vink, who reported that a "good death" means a death decided after clear and careful consideration with the individual's role as large as possible and carried out with the utmost care. Such a death would not be executed in forced loneliness and, if possible, would include contact with loved ones. The death would be self-determined and self-performed. Additionally, it would be without pain and suffering in dignified circumstances and be quick, peaceful, and quiet.

Dr. Vink also cites some lethal medications which I have omitted, and offers some cautions about possible obstacles and dangers, such as a zealous public prosecutor, wrong medications, wrong procedure.

And the following is from the *British Medical Journal*:

**Principles of a good death:**

- To know when death is coming, and to understand what can be expected
- To be able to retain control of what happens
- To be afforded dignity and privacy
- To have control over pain relief and other symptom control
- To have choice and control over where death occurs (at home or elsewhere)
- To have access to information and expertise of whatever kind is necessary
- To have access to any spiritual or emotional support required
- To have access to hospice care in any location, not only in hospital
- To have control over who is present and who shares the end
- To be able to issue advance directives which ensure wishes are respected
- To have time to say goodbye, and control over other aspects of timing
- To be able to leave when it is time to go, and not to have life prolonged pointlessly.

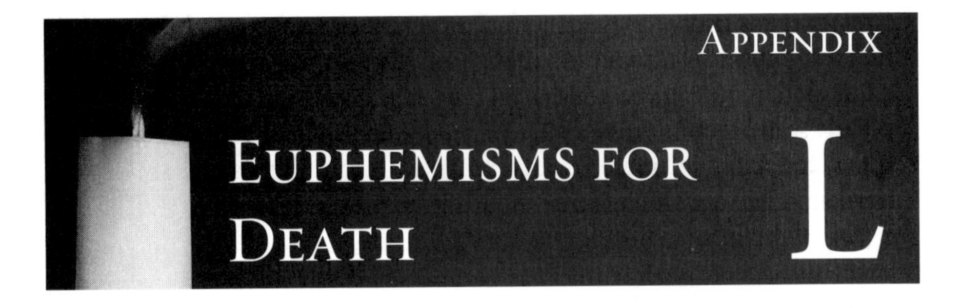

# Appendix L
# Euphemisms for Death

## Understanding our Death Language may Improve Understanding of our Death Attitudes

Using euphemisms, metaphors and slang terms instead of death and dying terms is not always undesirable. Sometimes this alternative death language can help with the healing process. Consider how much easier it is to cope with a death if one thinks of the deceased person as having fallen asleep, found an everlasting peace or merely passing or fading away. Other times the alternative death language is amusing, part of black humor — the interweaving of macabre or horrid events with humorous or farcical ones. Still in other situations death slang or euphemisms are used as a coping or a distancing strategy.

Many of the professions that deal with people who are dead or dying on a daily basis, such as emergency medical systems, physicians, nurses and funeral professionals, utilize black humor as one of the strategies to cope with the stressors of the profession.

In any language, it seems, the lexicon of death will be tremendously nuanced. It's a subject that lends itself to euphemization or softening, but also to earthy idioms that might defuse some of the anxieties surrounding death.

We could start with Mark Twain, who included a vignette in his 1872 book *Roughing It* recounting a conversation between a "stalwart rough" in Nevada and a well-spoken clergyman:

> "You see, one of the boys has gone up the flume—"
> "Gone where?"
> "Up the flume—throwed up the sponge, you understand."
> "Thrown up the sponge?"
> "Yes—kicked the bucket—"
> "Ah—has departed to that mysterious country from whose bourne no traveler returns."
> "Return! I reckon not. Why pard, he's dead!"

The juxtaposition of unsentimental expressions like "kicked the bucket" and the clergyman's flowery alternative wonderfully demonstrates that simple talk of "dying" can be avoided by language both high and low.

Nearly a century later, in 1969, *Monty Python's Flying Circus* aired their famous "dead parrot" sketch, which includes this unforgettable rant by John Cleese as a frustrated customer who has bought a dead-on-arrival parrot from a pet shop:

> 'E's not pinin'! 'E's passed on! This parrot is no more! He has ceased to be! 'E's expired and gone to meet 'is maker! 'E's a stiff! Bereft of life, 'e rests in peace! If you hadn't nailed 'im to the perch 'e'd be pushing up the daisies! 'Is metabolic processes are now 'istory! 'E's off the twig! 'E's kicked the bucket, 'e's shuffled off 'is mortal coil, run down the curtain and joined the bleedin' choir invisible!! This is an ex-parrot!

Here is my list of euphemisms that I've collected for years. These are words and phrases used to avoid using "D" words like dead, dying, died, die. Some others skirt direct talk about death and dying such as denoting the final resting place rather than call it a grave. Yes, some expressions contain "D" words but are accompanied by additional descriptors. Others are simply quite uncommon terms. And some are dysphemisms, humorous, or sardonic. Some come from specific groups, such as technical writers, computer programmers. cooks, religion, Internet, writers, criminals, sports, or *Star Trek*.

1 person chamber
15 minutes of flame
20,000 bodies into the past
404ever, pulse not found
6 foot death trap
7 steps to heaven
a little folding of the hands to sleep
a little slumber
a place below that reminds us of above
a place in the sun
a real deadbeat
a stiff
achieving warp zero
adios park
after limbo
after the last chance
all souls camp
allow natural death (AND)
among the angels
an awfully big adventure
an improvement over technical writing
and it has 7 steps
angels ways
answer the last call
apparently out!-house
ash can
assigned to the hale bopp project
assumed room temperature
at the end of one's rope
Avalon
avenue of souls
awaiting an organized letter campaign
awake to life immortal
bad shot's reunion
barrow
basting the formaldehyde turkey
be all over with one
be dead as a door nail
be gathered to one's fathers
be no more
beam me up, God-y!
become plant fertilizer
beehive tomb
beinhaus
beneath the shade tree
bereft of life
big sleep
bit the dust
bite it
bite the big one
bite the biscuit
bless the world with one's heels
body barters
body dump
body humidifier

body park
boldly going, going, gone
bone garden
bone ground
bone house
bone orchard
boneyard bonanza
bonezone
boogey land
booked on a cruise on the dirt submarine
boot hill
bought a pine condo
bought a Yugo
bought his lunch
bought the boxa
bought the farm
breathe one's last
bucket kicking carnival
butt can
cadaverburg
called home
captive audience
carcass cache
carrion heaven
cash in your chips
cash out
cashed in his chips
castle grayskull
catch one's end
caught the big anvil
cease to breathe
cease to live
celestial discharge
cement tree
checked into the motel deep 6
checked into the wooden Waldorf
checked out
chillin' with Walt
city of angels
city of eternal rest
city of forever peace
city of the damned
city of the doomed
city of the silent
clicked the bucket
climb the eternally long stairwell
climb the golden stair
close one's eyes
coffinteria
coiled up his ropes
cold feet village
cold storage
collapsed his/her outline
come to an untimely end
come to dust
community gallows
community of decay
compost container
compost heap
condition non-conducive to life
cooking for the Kennedys
corpse city
corpse condos
corpseway
created an opening on shuffleboard court three
croaked
cross on the Stygian ferry
cross ranch
cross the bar
cross the great divide
crossed to the other side
crossing the bar
crossing the river
crow station
crow-bait farm
crypt of the dead
crypt of zombies
curled up his toes
curtains
cwoaked (Elmer Fudd)
daisy patch
daisy pushin' patch
dance floor for the last horizontal tango
dance on air
dancing the hokey croakey
dangle in the sheriff's picture frame
dark carnival
dark dance floor
dark grounds of doom
darkness
dating Bambi's mom
Davey Jone's parlor
Davey Jones's locker
d'dants farm
dead as a dodo
dead as a doornail
dead center
dead domain
dead man's party
dead people's place
dead silence
dead zone
deadbangers ball
dead-end
deanimate
dearly departed
death suite
death's bedroom
death's castle
death's domain
death's door
death's doorway
death's gate
death's parlor
death's playground
debt we all must pay
decay buffet
deceased
decedent
decomposers notes at rest
deep 6 garden
deep six
deep sixed
deleted from the BOM
depart this life
departed
departed from this world
departed line
depository
desfile de tumbas
deterioration chamber
devil's house
devil's playground

devil's soulmine
devil's tomb
dew drop dead inn
did... go... all... the... way!
dirt bed
dirt discotheque
dirt dorm
dirt nap
dirt of souls
dirt vaults
dirty yellow submarine
disassemble
disincorporate
dispatched
do not resuscitate (DNR)
documented the big d
doggy digs
doing the burlap backstroke (Garfield)
doing the long limbo
doing the pine-box lambada
doing the Vulcan ground meld
doing the worm wave at stiff stadium
donating the liver paté
done like dinner
doom
doonesburied
doorway between worlds
down under
downtime
dozin' dozens
Dr. Frankenstein's "farm"-acy
drop into the grave
drop off
drop off the twig
drop off this mortal coil
dungeon of the damned
dust bin
dust factory
dust to dust
dust to dust reunion
dwelling of the dead
E. T. bone home
earthsuit closet
earthy bed
earwig farm
eating a dirt sandwich
eating a moss muffin
empty case case
end of the line
end of the material line
end one's days
end one's earthly career
end one's life
endless vacationland
endsville
eternal care facility
eternal damnation
eternal hangover
eternal home
eternal resting place
eternal vacation
eternity's foyer
etherworld
ex-human
expired
exported to a flat file
express elevator to hell
face-planting the meringue
faded away
failure to meet their wellness potential
falling downhill at top speed
feed the fishes
fenced in hollow ground
fertilizer square
fettuccine al dead-o
fiddler's green
field of screams
final quiet
final residence
final resting place
final snoozing place
flatline
flying the marble kite
for whom the bell tolls
forever city
formatted with black borders
fossil farm
Frankenstein's workshop
Freddy's hangout
free sex for those who dig
free worm food
freedom
freeing the spirit
full of farmers
garden of lost souls
garden of remembrance
garden of rest
garden of serenity
garden of shadows
garden of silence
garden of sleep
garden of souls
garden of stones
garden of the sleepers
gargoyle garage
gate of life
gate to the dream world you've waited for
gateway to Hades
gave up the ghost
get knocked off
get pasted
get smeared
get toasted
get your halo
ghost town
ghostyard
gibbed
give an obolus to Charon
give up the ghost
go for a burton
go home feet first
go home in a box
go off
go off the hooks
go out like the snuff of a candle
go tatty-bye
go the way of all earth
go the way of all flesh
go to a necktie party
go to Abraham's bosom
go to heaven

go to meet one's maker
go to one's just reward
go to one's last account
go to one's last home
go to one's long account
go to one's rest
go to the happy hunting ground
go to the last roundup
go to the wall
God's holy grounds
God's playground
God's resting place
going into the fertilizer business
going to the slab prom
golf course where everyone gets a hole in one
Golgotha
gone
gone home
gone on to his reward
gone out with the tide
gone to a better place
gone to Jesus
gone to meet his maker
gone to meet the majority
gone to the big glass house in the sky
gone to the big sleep
gone to the world of light
got her/his final reward
got some skybox tickets
got whacked
gottesacker
grateful dead
had his lot
had his/her 80-column card punched
hades dominion
hade's half-acre
hades' home
hade's playground
hallowed ground
hand in one's checks
hand in one's chips
hang up your tack
hanging 10 on the satin-lined surfboard
hard as a carp
harvest of souls
has reservations at the chateau eternity
has run down the curtain to join the choir invisible
haunt spot
haunting hollow
he scores! he shoots! he ODs!
headstone gallery
headstone park
heads-up club
hearse pit-stop
heavenly haven
heaven's door
heaven's gate
his lot has ceased to be
his number's up
Hong Kong phooeyed
hop the twig
horizontal Hilton
hotel California
house of nothing
I told you I was sick
I willed my life away
Ichabod's isle
immortally challenged
in a tapered tanning booth
in the marble mailbox
in the sweet hereafter
in the tightly sealed tanning booth
information superhighway roadkill
inhumation
inspired a new warning message
installed the Kevorkian plug-n-play
interment ground
invested in PointCast
is no more
isolation chamber
it doesn't matter whether you've got mail
it's life but not as we know it
it's Taps
jockeying for position in the dirt derby
John Doe's haven
join one's ancestors
join the angels
join the greater number
join the majority
just add maggots
kaput
Kavorkian's trophy case
kick the can
kicked the bucket
kicked the oxygen habit
kind nature's signal of retreat
kiss the dust
knockin' on heaven's door
land of no return
land of the dead
landscapes of granite ghosts
last exit to Brooklyn
last gasp saloon
last lounge
last lovers' lane
last pit stop on the highway of life
last plantation
last safety deposit box
last sleep
last stand
last stop
last stop to paradise
last time-out
lateral mobility
launched into eternity
lay down one's life
left the building
lich-gate
lining the bird cage
living-challenged
living-impaired

locked and loaded
lonely SDF (solo dead figure)
long barrow
lose one's life
losers club
lost collection of mortals
lost in translation
lost souls of today
made the big deadline
maggot munchkinland
maggot tunnels
mailed in his warranty card
make one's will
making a call from the horizontal phone booth
mamma always said, life is like a row of coffins, never one will fit
marble mall
marble orchard
marble ranch
marinating in soil and worms
marking the bronze by shopping at the mahogany mini mall
married to OJ
matter check-in post
McCemetery
meat
meet one's death
meet one's end
meet one's maker
meet the Reaper
met the grim beep-beeper
metabolically challenged
Midian
miracle hair salon 'n' nails
Morrison hotel
mortal world's exit
mortician's scorepad
most popular place in town
motel deep 6
motel eternity
mother nature's acres
moved into upper management
murder victims anonymous
my peaceful escape
mystical world
narrow house
nastalgia
necrophiliac heaven
necrophiliac singles bar
needin' a nap
negative patient care outcome
netherworld
never ending dirt bath
never ending party
never never land
never-ending trip
nevermore
night's Plutonian shore
no brain hotel
no longer able to view the web's hottest women
no longer eligible for the census
now you're f#$@ed!
obituary mambo club
off the record
oh no,,, oh no,,,
OJ's house
old crow's nest
on a one way trip
on one's last legs
on permanent holodeck duty
on the bier
on the hell express
on the road to nowhere
on the sod subway
on the unable to breathe list
organic rot fest
osteo-poe-row-styx
out of business
parking place
pass in one's checks
pass in one's chips
pass over Jordan
passed
passed away
passed on
past people plantation
pastures of peace
pauper's hill
pay the debt to nature
pay the piper
peasant under grass
peg out
perished
permanent retirement park
permanent vacation
permanently out of print
picking up your harp
place of doom
place of eternal darkness
place of eternal rest
place of interment
place of judgment
place of nirvana
place of no return
place of peace
place of rest
place of the final sleep
place where the sun don't shine
playground for the undead
playing harp duets with Hoffa
playing in the subterranean sand box
please kill me - whoops, too late
Pluto's vacation yard
point of no return
polyandrium
pop off
pop off the hooks
portal between worlds
printed white on white
procrastinator's paradise
prolonged sleep
promoted to subterranean truffle Inspector
pull the plug

pulling a Spock without a Planet Genesis to back It up
pumping lid
purgatorial preparation place
pushin' up parsley
pushing up daisies
pushing up miss daisy
pushing up parking lot
pushing up posies
put in the crisper
put on immortality
put on the wooden overcoat
quietly slipped from our embrace
really stuck her dismount
Reaper's paradise
receive one's final warrant
reformatted
reformatted by God
relinquish one's life
remaindered
renting the grass tuxedo
repose depot
resign one's being
resign one's breath
resign one's life
rest home for the damned
rest in peace
resting
resting grounds
resting place
rests in peace
retroactive abortion
ride the lightning
riding a satin pony
riding the perma-pine
riding the soil sidecar
rigga bell if mortis wakes up
RIP central
roach motel
rorschached
rottenskull cafe
Rottingham
rubbed out
ruh-roh'ed
rung down the curtain and joined the choir invisible
salon of souls
sampling the French Onion Soup with a salmonella spoon
Satan's tools
Scooby-Done
scrap heap of souls
sent to the dirt archives
sepulchral cist
serving a major in the pine penalty box
SFU express (six feet under express)
shadowlands
shaft tomb
shed the mortal coil
shit the bed
shouldn't have sniffed that last line
showing St. Peter her sports bra
shrouded souls -n- dirt
shuffle off this mortal coil
signing for the lower me down bouquet
singing with the angels
single room flat
single unit morphing station
sink into the dirt
six feet under
sleep city
sleep of transition
sleep with the fishes
sleephole
sleepin' single
sleeps with the tribbles
slip one's cable
slowly cooling to room temperature
slug sucking apartment complex
slumber site for souls
smoked
smorgasbord of decay
snuff it
solarium
solitary confinement
solo flight
somebody off the record
soul garden
soul patch
souls last domain
soul's morgue
south of the frostline
sowing the Elysian fields
spawn pit
specter's hectare
spirit's playground
spiritsville
splitsville
spook nook
stable of the pale horse
stairway to heaven
stairway to hell
standing in line at the sod sizzler
stationary vehicle
staying at club mud
step onto one's last bus
step out
stiff city
stiff slumber
stone dead
stone orchard
stoned
storage space
street pizza
struck out by the big blue pencil
stuffed
stupa
succumbed
summer lands
sun one's moccasins
surrender one's life
tailgating with Jesus
take a dirt nap
take an earth bath
take one's last sleep
take the last count

taken out of production
taking a phone call from President Taft
taking a spin in the brass-handled sedan
taking acting lessons from Shatner
taking minutes for the Maker
taking the dirt nap
taking the final curtain
terminated
termination
termination station
test driving the wooden Buick
that dreamless sleep
that fell arrest which summons the all without bail
that fell sergeant
that good night
that grim ferryman
that was all she wrote
the angels' enchanted gardens
the big jump
the bosom of the father and his God
the bottom line
the breath is out of the body
the couch of dreamless sleep
the crown of life
the crypt of doom
the dark lord's palace
the downward path
the dread abode
the drop-dead-fred bed
the dungeon
the empty vessel
the ending of lifecycles
the eternal nap
the eternal offsite assignment
the eternal pit
the eternal room
the eternal sleep of no escape
the eternal yawn
the fat lady has sung
the final destination
the final edit
the garden of forever
the gates of the underworld
the gateway to eternity
the granite garden
the grave closes over one
the great
the great below
the great beyond
the great leveler
the groundhog's den
the Hamlet sleep
the happy bouncie hunting ground of doom
the hill
the holding pen
the hollow lands
the human egress
the inevitable hour
the inn of the wandering souls
the journey's end
the king of terrors
the latter end
the lone couch of this everlasting sleep
the medieval zone
the notorious D.O.A.
the other realm
the pale priest of the mute people
the people landfill
the place of the spirits
the place where grampy lives
the place where time stops
the raven's haven
the real graveyard shift
the records of the day the man did fall
the safest place in the world
the seamouth of mortality
the sleeping partner of life
the tax shelter
the terminal
the undiscovered country
the up to 10000 and still counting knockout
the valley of the souls
the waiting room
the wife's trophy case
the wooden bed
the world beyond
threefold return
threshold to eternity
time sharing the oblong condo
tipping the dirt maitre' d
to be continued
to blink for an excessive amount of time
to push up daisies
to thine own world be dead
toes up
toes up lot
tomb
tomb of the dead
tomb town
tombstone
too dark park
took the ol' kryptonite suppository
tope
toss in one's alley
total relaxation
tower of silence
toxic lock-up
traded to the angels
transcended
transferred to the U.S.S. Oblivion
transferred to *www.hasbecome.com/post*
transition chamber
translated into glory
transmutation chamber

trench
tribute due unto nature
trolling for topsoil trout
trunk
turn one's face to the wall
turn to dust
turn up one's toes
turning up daisies
umbra
underground condo
underground hotel
underworld
unmovable spot
untimely end
Valhalla
valley of death
valley of the dead
valley of the kings
vault
v-chipped!
vermin village
very, very passive voice
village of the darned
Virginia's vault
vis a vis the metabolic processes
visiting Davy Jones' locker
visiting Shatner's hair
visiting the chat tomb
volleyball court where everyone gets a dig
vultures' reason for starvation
walked the plank
was a goner
was beamed up
was done in
was taken
wasted
wasted space
watch-where-you-step land
watery grave
wear a glass necklace
wearing a Columbian necktie
wearing concrete galoshes
wearing the toe-tag turtleneck
wedding day with the worms
went online
went to a new life
went to his/her eternal reward
went to see the fat lady in concert
went to that big spell checker in the sky
what do you want on your tombstone?
when the fat lady sings
winning one for The Reaper
witches' playpen
with the angels
withered away
worm buffet
worm condo
worm eating
worm farm
worm food
worm pit
worm trough
worm work farm
wormhole
wormpatch
worms night out
worm's restaurant
worst place to hold a necrophiliacs anonymous meeting
*www.he's-dead-jim.com*
*www.myfirstcoronary.com*
yard of farewells
ye old fossil collection
yield one's breath
yield up the ghost
your arms are too short to box with God
your tax dollars at work
you're kidding me, right
zeroing out the tricorder
zombie hang out
zombie inn
zombie insane asylum
zombie land
zombie playground
zombie zone
zombie zoo

# About the Author

An Episcopal priest and thanatologist, John Abraham has devoted most of his adult life as a pioneer in the fields of grief therapy, hospice, death education, and, more controversially, the right-to-die movement.

This book is a product of those years of experience. Rabbi Earl A. Grollman, perhaps America's best-known authority of death education and grief therapy, comments that "Whatever your opinions on the right-to-die movement, this is a book you must have in your library."

Abraham is also well-known for his sometimes unconventional sense of humor; perhaps personified by the snapshot on this page with his coffin, which serves as a bookcase pending its future use. His wit makes it easier for people to become educated on a serious subject, to be better prepared for their own eventual deaths and to advocate for their loved ones at the end of life.

John is a graduate of The Peddie School, Colgate University, and Virginia Theological Seminary and a lifetime member of The Association for Death Education and Counseling through which he earned his advanced certification as a Fellow in Thanatology. He is also a lifetime member of all U.S. right-to-die organizations and has served with numerous groups long championing minorities and the underdog. His primary avocations are reading, tennis, and — having enjoyed about a dozen motorcycles — he recently gave up riding a "suicycle."

The Reverend Abraham frequently gives talks and workshops on issues relating to death, grief, and the right-to-die movement. His personal Web site is: *www.JohnLAbraham.com*. He may be contacted directly through the information on that site, or through the publisher, Upper Access Books, *info@upperaccess.com*.